Computer Interfacing

To my wife, Olive Louisa

Computer Interfacing

George A. Smith, B.A.(Hons), C.Eng., M.I.E.E.

Newnes

OXFORD AUCKLAND BOSTON JOHANNESBURG MELBOURNE NEW DELHI

Newnes
An imprint of Butterworth-Heinemann
Linacre House, Jordan Hill, Oxford OX2 8DP
225 Wildwood Avenue, Woburn, MA 01801-2041
A division of Reed Educational and Professional Publishing Ltd

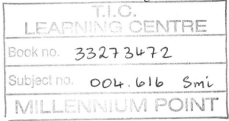 A member of the Reed Elsevier plc group

First published 2000

British Library Cataloguing in Publication Data
A catalogue record for this book is available from the British Library.

ISBN 0 7506 4474 5

Library of Congress Cataloguing in Publication Data
A catalogue record for this book is available from the Library of Congress.

Data manipulation by David Gregson Associates, Beccles, Suffolk
Printed and bound in Great Britain

PLANT A
TREE

British Trust for
Conservation Volunteers

FOR EVERY TITLE THAT WE PUBLISH, BUTTERWORTH-HEINEMANN
WILL PAY FOR BTCV TO PLANT AND CARE FOR A TREE.

Contents

Introduction

This book has been written with two main aims, the first of which is to provide students with an understanding of microprocessor-based systems and their use in instrumentation, control and communications. The second aim is to encourage Electronic Engineering students to carry out practical exercises and projects, involving the development of both hardware and software.

The interfacing exercises described use the high level language C, and have been developed on a personal computer (PC). The hardware generally consists of a few ICs, which may be plugged into proto-board or soldered onto strip-board. The exercise development objectives were first, to use the minimum amount of hardware, and second, to make the C programs as readable as possible.

Chapters 8, 9, 10, 11 and 12 all contain basic exercises in which both the software and hardware are fully described. These exercises are designed to introduce students to interfacing from a PC using simple programs and hardware. All the basic exercises have been developed and tested by the author. Many of them are developments of exercises used for teaching BTEC Interfacing and Electronics courses to BT apprentices at Suffolk College. Following the basic exercises there are suggestions for further developments, some of which may be turned into full-scale projects.

The exercises neither require a great deal of memory nor do they need to be performed at high speed, so a PC with a 286 processor will be perfectly adequate.

The fourteen chapters have three distinctive sections:

Part One: Chapters 1 to 3 are mainly intended for revision and references.

Part Two   Chapters 4 to 7 form a theoretical section, although Chapter 5 does contain some project ideas.

Part Three   Chapters 8 to 14 are interfacing exercises.
              Chapter 8 introduces interfacing via the serial port.
              Chapters 9 to 11 contain many exercises using a programmable peripheral interface.
              Chapter 12 repeats suitable exercises described in Chapters 9 to 11 but using the parallel printer port. In some cases the software has been modified to introduce new ideas.

Chapter 13 contains further exercises which could be developed into projects.

Chapter 14 includes a selection of test equipment, some ideas on testing, descriptions of hardware and a selection of hardware and software problems.

The interfacing exercises require both the development of short C programs and the construction of fairly basic logic circuits. When making connections to computers it is essential that the following procedure is adopted:

 (i) Test the circuit before connecting it to the computer.
 (ii) Ask a competent person to check both the circuit and the computer connections.
(iii) Make sure that the computer is switched OFF when connecting or disconnecting circuits.
(iv) Avoid bending plug pins by making sure that plugs or sockets are pushed in straight.
 (v) Observe the computer when it is switched ON to ensure that it runs up correctly.

The connections and information are given in good faith, but the author cannot be held responsible for damage to equipment, and, although unlikely, injury to any person carrying out exercises described in this book.

Many thanks to Mike Tooley for his support during the development of this book, and to the following companies for allowing me to include extracts from their publications:

Intel Corporation (UK) Ltd
Motorola Semiconductor Products Sector
Philips Semiconductors Inc.
Zilog Inc.

Part One
Revision and Reference

1 Number systems

This chapter contains a review of number systems used in digital computers. Two-state logic devices, which are the building blocks of digital computers, require binary signals for their operation.

Unlike normal arithmetic, using pen and paper, number manipulation by an electronic system must be designed to handle a fixed length of binary digits (bits), typically a byte of 8 bits, a word of 16 bits, or a long word of 32 bits.

1.1 Direct conversion of binary numbers

Each bit of a binary number has an equivalent denary weighting. The least significant bit (LSB) of a binary integer is 2^0, and each bit to the left increases by a power of 2, see Figure 1.1. Figure 1.2 shows the equivalent

Bit x	7	6	5	4	3	2	1	0
2^x	128	64	32	16	8	4	2	1

Figure 1.1   Weighting of bits for integers

Bit x	−1	−2	−3	−4	−5	−6	−7	−8
2^x	0.5	0.25	0.125	0.0625	0.031 25	0.015 625	0.007 812 5	0.003 906 3

Figure 1.2   Weighting of bits for numbers less than 1

denary value of bits for numbers less than 1, where each bit to the right decreases by a power of 2.

1.1.1   Converting from denary to binary

One method of converting numbers from denary to binary is shown in the example below.

Example (a)   Convert 44_{10} to 8 bit binary:

Method: Subtract the next lowest bit weighting (Figure 1.1) from the number and then from the remainder:

		Bit weighting	7 128	6 64	5 32	4 16	3 8	2 4	1 2	0 1
Number	44									
	-32				1					
Remainder	12									
	-8						1			
Remainder	4									
	-4							1		
Remainder	0									
		Binary No.	0	0	1	0	1	1	0	0

Answer: $44_{10} = 00101100_2$

1.1.2   Converting from binary to denary

This process may be simply carried out by adding the bit weighting for each 1 in the binary number, as shown in the example below.

Example (b)   Convert 10001111_2 to denary:

Bit weighting	7 128	6 64	5 32	4 16	3 8	2 4	1 2	0 1	Sum
Number	1	0	0	0	1	1	1	1	
Value	128				8	4	2	1	143

Answer: $10001111_2 = 143_{10}$

1.2 Binary coded decimal (BCD)

An alternative way of using binary to represent denary numbers is to provide each digit (0 to 9) of a denary number with a binary code. 4-bit binary codes are the minimum required to represent numbers 0 to 9. The table in Figure 1.3 shows several different ways of arranging 10 combinations of 4 bits. It also shows the 2-out-of-5 code, which gives error protection[1].

Digit	8421	2421	XS3	Gray	2-out-of-5
0	0000	0000	0011	0000	11000
1	0001	0001	0100	0001	00011
2	0010	0010	0101	0011	00101
3	0011	0011	0110	0010	00110
4	0100	0100	0111	0110	01001
5	0101	1011	1000	1110	01010
6	0110	1100	1001	1010	01100
7	0111	1101	1010	1011	10001
8	1000	1110	1011	1001	10010
9	1001	1111	1100	1000	10100

Figure 1.3   BCD numbering systems

Comments on Figure 1.3;

(i)   8421 is natural binary code.
(ii)   2421 reduces the value of a single bit error from 8 to 4.
(iii)   XS3 is a code with a probability of 1 equal to the probability of 0. Note there is no 0000 codeword.
(iv)   Gray code has a sequence of code words which all have a distance[2] of one. This reduces the possibility of errors from some mechanical transducers.
(v)   2-out-of-5 will detect one error as all code words must contain two 1s.

1.3 Hexadecimal numbers (hex)

A simple way of expressing binary numbers is to convert them to base-16 known as hexadecimal (hex) numbers, where each hex symbol represents 4bits, see Figure 1.4. Sixteen symbols are required for hexadecimal numbers, 0 to 9 are used to represent numbers 0 to 9 and A to F (lower or upper case) to represent 10 to 15 respectively.

[1] If there are not two 1s in a received code word, there is an error, and the word is rejected.
[2] Distance is the number of different bits between a pair of code words. The following pairs of code words all have a distance of one.

0100	1100	111101010
0000	1101	101101010

Figure 1.4 shows the relationship of numbers from 0 to 20_{10} to their binary, hexadecimal and BCD equivalents. The numbers at the top of columns indicate the weighting of the digits in that column.

Denary base-10 10 1	Binary base-2 16 8 4 2 1	Hexadecimal base-12 16 1	Binary coded Decimal (BCD) tens 8 4 2 1	units 8 4 2 1
0 0	0 0 0 0 0	0 0	0 0 0 0	0 0 0 0
0 1	0 0 0 0 1	0 1	0 0 0 0	0 0 0 1
0 2	0 0 0 1 0	0 2	0 0 0 0	0 0 1 0
0 3	0 0 0 1 1	0 3	0 0 0 0	0 0 1 1
0 4	0 0 1 0 0	0 4	0 0 0 0	0 1 0 0
0 5	0 0 1 0 1	0 5	0 0 0 0	0 1 0 1
0 6	0 0 1 1 0	0 6	0 0 0 0	0 1 1 0
0 7	0 0 1 1 1	0 7	0 0 0 0	0 1 1 1
0 8	0 1 0 0 0	0 8	0 0 0 0	1 0 0 0
0 9	0 1 0 0 1	0 9	0 0 0 0	1 0 0 1
1 0	0 1 0 1 0	0 A	0 0 0 1	0 0 0 0
1 1	0 1 0 1 1	0 B	0 0 0 1	0 0 0 1
1 2	0 1 1 0 0	0 C	0 0 0 1	0 0 1 0
1 3	0 1 1 0 1	0 D	0 0 0 1	0 0 1 1
1 4	0 1 1 1 0	0 E	0 0 0 1	0 1 0 0
1 5	0 1 1 1 1	0 F	0 0 0 1	0 1 0 1
1 6	1 0 0 0 0	1 0	0 0 0 1	0 1 1 0
1 7	1 0 0 0 1	1 1	0 0 0 1	0 1 1 1
1 8	1 0 0 1 0	1 2	0 0 0 1	1 0 0 0
1 9	1 0 0 1 1	1 3	0 0 0 1	1 0 0 1
2 0	1 0 1 0 0	1 4	0 0 1 0	0 0 0 0

Figure 1.4   Number relationships

1.4   Signed numbers

There is often a need to indicate the sign of a number. Unlike written numbers, where the + or − sign is placed to the left, in a digital system the sign must be part of the binary code. There are again several methods of achieving this, one of which is described below. In general the most significant bit (MSB), the bit on the left-hand end of the binary code, is used as a sign bit, 0 representing positive and 1 representing negative numbers.

Example (c)   There are a total of 2^8 ($=256$) binary combinations in an 8-bit system. The binary combinations from 00000000 to 01111111 represent denary positive numbers from 0 to 127 (0 to 7F hex). This leaves binary combinations from 10000000 to 11111111 to represent negative numbers.

The 2's complement method of representing negative numbers is described here.

1.4.1 2's complement representation of negative numbers

Negative number coding is achieved by using the following three steps:

(i) Convert the magnitude of the number to binary in the normal way.
(ii) Complement the resulting binary number. That is, replace 0s with 1s and 1s with 0s.
(iii) Add 1 to the least significant bit (LSB).

To find the denary value of any binary number with a 1 as the MSB.

(i) Complement the binary number. That is, replace 0s with 1s and 1s with 0s.
(ii) Add 1 to the least significant bit (LSB).
(iii) Convert the resulting binary number back to denary in the normal way.

Figure 1.5 shows how denary numbers are represented in an 8-bit system which uses 2's complement for negative numbers

Denary	Binary	Hexadecimal
0	0000 0000	0 0
1	0000 0001	0 1
127	0111 1111	7 F
−128	1000 0000	8 0
−1	1111 1111	F F

Figure 1.5 8-bit signed number range

Example (d) Represent -1 in 2's complement 8-bit binary:

(i) Convert to binary $1_{10} = 0000\ 0001$
(ii) Complement $= 1111\ 1110$
(iii) Add 1 to LSB $= 1111\ 1111 = \underline{FF\ hex}$ Answer

Example (e) Represent -127 in 8-bit binary.

(i) Convert to binary $127_{10} = 0111\ 1111$
(ii) Complement $= 1000\ 0000$
(iii) Add 1 to LSB $= 1000\ 0001 = \underline{81\ hex}$ Answer

Note $-128_{10} = 1000\ 0000_2$ (80 hex), cannot be obtained by the above method as there is no $+128_{10}$ in this system.

Example (f) Find the denary value of 9A hex.

(i) Convert to binary $9A_{16} = 1001\ 1010$ binary
(ii) Complement $= 0110\ 0101$
(iii) Add 1 to the LSB $= 0110\ 0110$
     Convert to denary $= \underline{-102_{10}}$ Answer

1.4.2   Addition of signed binary numbers

Example (g)   Calculate $7_{10} + 90_{10}$.

(i)	Convert 7 to binary	0000 0111
(ii)	Convert 90 to binary	0101 1010
		0110 0001 $= 97_{10}$ Answer

Example (h)   Calculate $-7_{10} - 90_{10}$.

This sum may be rewritten in the form $-7 + (-90)$

(i)	Convert 7 to binary	0000 0111
(ii)	Complement	1111 1000
(iii)	Add 1	$-7 = $ 1111 1001 $\rightarrow$ 1111 1001
(iv)	Convert 90 to binary	0101 1010
(v)	Complement	1010 0101
(vi)	Add 1	$-90 = $ 1010 0110 $\rightarrow$ 1010 1110
	Result	$-97_{10} = $ 1001 1111
	Final carry discarded	1

Example (i)   Calculate $47_{10} + 90_{10}$.

(i)	Convert 47 to binary	0010 1111
(ii)	Convert 90 to binary	0101 1010
		1000 1001 $=$ Overflow error Answer

An overflow error occurs if the addition of two positive numbers gives a negative answer, or the addition of two negative numbers gives a positive result.

1.5   Floating point numbers

The floating point numbers format is required to cater for very large and very small numbers. Each floating point number has two fields, a **mantissa** and an **exponent**. Positive or negative numbers are represented by a positive or negative mantissa respectively. Numbers greater than 1 are represented by a positive exponent and numbers less than 1 by a negative exponent.

To give the maximum resolution the binary point is moved to the left of the most significant 1 in the mantissa. When the number is normalised in this manner there is no need to store the most significant 1. All bits go to zero if the number is zero. To achieve greater resolution an option to lengthen the mantissa may be included. Figure 1.6 shows a 32-bit floating point format. The mantissa is normalised and hence there is an *implied* 1 to the left of bit 23 except when the number is zero.

Mantissa sign	Exponent	Mantissa
31	30....................24	23..0

.1 Implied, between bits 23 and 24, when number is not zero

Figure 1.6 Floating point format

1.5.1 Floating point conversion examples

Example (j) Convert 12387_{10} to floating point format.

(i) Convert to hex   = 3063 hex

(ii) Convert to binary   = 0011 0000 0110 0011

(iii) To find the value of the *mantissa* move the binary point to the left, placing it in front of the most significant 1, in this case 14 places.
$$= .11\ 0000\ 0110\ 0011$$
The value of the *exponent* is equal to the number of places moved by the binary point. In this case 14.

(iv) Convert 14 to binary for the exponent
$$= 0001110$$

(v) The sign of the mantissa is positive.

The floating point number, using the format given in Figure 1.6 is:

<u>0 000 1110 1000 0011 0001 1000 0000 0000</u>

↑

.1 Implied

1.5.2 Biased exponents

In some systems a bias number is added to the exponent so that all exponents are positive. This provides for greater ease in comparing exponents during calculations. In the following examples a bias of 63 is added to the exponents.

Example (k) Convert -120_{10} to floating point format.

(i) Binary value   = 111 1000

(ii) Move the binary point to the left 7 places   .1111000

(iii) Exponent $= 7 + 63 = 70$

(iv) Convert exponent to binary   1000110

(v) Sign of mantissa is negative   = 1

(vi) Floating point number

<u>1 100 0110 1110 0000 0000 0000 0000 0000</u>

↑

.1 Implied

Example (1)   Convert 0.04_{10} to floating point format.

(i) Find the base 2 exponent of the number to be converted

$$\text{exponent}^3 = \log_2(0.04)$$
$$= -4.64$$
$$\text{round to integer} = -4$$

$$\text{biased exponent} = -4 + 63$$
$$= 59$$
$$= 0111011$$

(ii) Find the mantissa by dividing the number by 2^{exponent}

$$\text{Hence mantissa} = \frac{0.04}{2^{-4}}$$
$$= 0.64$$

(iii) Convert .64 to binary $= .10100010$

(iv) Sign is positive $= 0$

(v) Floating point number

$$0\ 011\ 1011\ 0100\ 0100\ 0000\ 0000\ 0000\ 0000$$

1.6 Representation of alphanumeric characters

ASCII (American Standard Code of Information Interchange) is the code generally used for representing alphanumeric characters, for communications between computers and printers, etc. This code had been used for many years in teleprinter communications.

There are a large number of control codes which enabled the transmitting teleprinter to directly control the receiving machine. All characters are encoded in a 7-bit code. An 8th bit, called a parity[4] bit, may be added to each code word as a simple error check. The 128 code words represent upper and lower case letters, numbers, additional symbols, and control codes. The ASCII codes are shown at the end of this chapter in tables in Figures 1.7 and 1.8.

1.7 Number system conversions

When using low level languages[5] it is often necessary to convert from, say, ASCII to decimal or hexadecimal and vice versa, or lower to upper case characters. There are numerous ways of achieving this, a few of which are shown below.

1.7.1 Convert all characters to upper case

The only difference between ASCII upper and lower case letters is bit 6 which is logic 0 for upper case and logic 1 for lower case. Hence to

---

[3] $\log_2 N = (\log_{10} N)/(\log_{10} 2)$.
[4] The parity bit may either be a 1 or a 0, the idea being to make the 1s in each code either odd or even.
[5] See Chapter 3 for an explanation of *low level languages*.

convert all characters to *upper* case logically AND[6] the ASCII code with binary mask 101 1111.

Example (m) Convert character to upper case.

$$\begin{array}{rl}
\text{Bit No.} & 7654321 \\
\text{ASCII d} = & 1100100 \\
\text{mask} = & \underline{1011111} \\
\text{AND each BIT pair} = & \overline{1000100} = \underline{\text{ASCII D} \quad \text{Answer}}
\end{array}$$

1.7.2 Convert all characters to lower case

In this case bit 6 must be converted to a logic 1 where necessary, so the ASCII code has to be logically ORed with the binary mask 010 0000.

Example (n) Convert character to lower case.

$$\begin{array}{rl}
\text{Bit No.} & 7654321 \\
\text{ASCII Y} = & 1011001 \\
\text{mask} = & \underline{0100000} \\
\text{OR each BIT pair} = & \overline{1111001} = \underline{\text{ASCII y} \quad \text{Answer}}
\end{array}$$

1.7.3 Convert ASCII 0 to 9 to 4-bit binary

Binary numbers 0 to 9 are obtained from bits 1, 2, 3 and 4 of ASCII codes 30 hex to 39 hex. So mask the ASCII code with a logical AND of 000 1111.

Example (o)

$$\begin{array}{rl}
\text{Bit No.} & 7654321 \\
\text{ASCII 7} = & 0110111 \\
\text{mask} = & \underline{0001111} \\
\text{AND each bit pair} = & \overline{0000111} = \underline{\text{Binary 7} \quad \text{Answer}}
\end{array}$$

1.7.4 Conversion of ASCII to hexadecimal

The conversion to hexadecimal numbers is a little inconvenient as A does not immediately follow 9. So a subtraction to make A to F represent 10 to 15 must be incorporated in the conversion process.

(i)   Convert letters to UPPER case.
(ii) Add 9 to the letters.
(iii) Convert to binary numbers.

---

[6] See Chapter 2 for an explanation of logic AND and OR.

Example (p) Convert ASCII b to bHex.

$$ASCII\ b = 1100010$$
$$Add\ 9 = \underline{0001001}$$
$$Result\quad \overline{1101011}$$
$$Mask\ with\ 0F\ hex = \underline{0001111}$$
$$\overline{0001011} = \underline{b\ Hex\quad Answer}$$

1.8 Questions

1 Add the following 8421 BCD numbers.

(a) 0100 0100 + 0011 0011
(b) 0010 1001 + 1001 1001
(c) 0101 0101 + 0111 1000

2 Complete the table below.

	Denary	Binary	Hex	8421 BCD
(a)	7	0000 0000 0111		
(b)		0000 0001 0001		0000 0001 0111
(c)		0000 0001 1011	0 1 D	
(d)	67			0000 0110 0111
(e)			0 6 5	0001 0000 0001
(f)	235	0000 1110 1011	0 E D	
(g)	428			0100 0010 1000

3 Convert 0.0000482 to floating point format.
4 Convert -0.312×10^{-8} to floating point format.
5 Convert the floating point number to denary

00000111 11001100 10101010 11110001.

Binary 7 6 5 4 3 2 1	Hex	Denary	Function abbreviation	Function description
0 0 0 0 0 0 0	0 0	0	NUL	Null
0 0 0 0 0 0 1	0 1	1	SOH	Start of Header
0 0 0 0 0 1 0	0 2	2	STX	Start of Text
0 0 0 0 0 1 1	0 3	3	ETX	End of Text
0 0 0 0 1 0 0	0 4	4	EOT	End of Transmission
0 0 0 0 1 0 1	0 5	5	ENQ	Enquiry
0 0 0 0 1 1 0	0 6	6	ACK	Acknowledge
0 0 0 0 1 1 1	0 7	7	BEL	Ring Bell
0 0 0 1 0 0 0	0 8	8	BS	Back Space
0 0 0 1 0 0 1	0 9	9	HT	Horizontal Tabulation
0 0 0 1 0 1 0	0 A	10	LF	Line Feed
0 0 0 1 0 1 1	0 B	11	VT	Vertical Tabulation
0 0 0 1 1 0 0	0 C	12	FF	Form Feed
0 0 0 1 1 0 1	0 D	13	CR	Carriage Return
0 0 0 1 1 1 0	0 E	14	SO	Shift Out
0 0 0 1 1 1 1	0 F	15	SI	Shift In
0 0 1 0 0 0 0	1 0	16	DLE	Data Link Escape
0 0 1 0 0 0 1	1 1	17	DC1	Device Control 1
0 0 1 0 0 1 0	1 2	18	DC2	Device Control 2
0 0 1 0 0 1 1	1 3	19	DC3	Device Control 3
0 0 1 0 1 0 0	1 4	20	DC4	Device Control 4
0 0 1 0 1 0 1	1 5	21	NAK	Negative Acknowledge
0 0 1 0 1 1 0	1 6	22	SYN	Synchronous Idle
0 0 1 0 1 1 1	1 7	23	ETB	End of Block
0 0 1 1 0 0 0	1 8	24	CAN	Cancel
0 0 1 1 0 0 1	1 9	25	EM	End of Medium
0 0 1 1 0 1 0	1 A	26	SUB	Substitute
0 0 1 1 0 1 1	1 B	27	ESC	Escape
0 0 1 1 1 0 0	1 C	28	FS	File Separator
0 0 1 1 1 0 1	1 D	29	GS	Group Separator
0 0 1 1 1 1 0	1 E	30	RS	Record Separator
0 0 1 1 1 1 1	1 F	31	US	Unit Separator
0 1 0 0 0 0 0	2 0	32	SP	Space
1 1 1 1 1 1 1	7 F	127	DEL	Delete

Figure 1.7   ASCII control codes

Binary 7654321	Hex	Den	Ch	Binary 7654321	Hex	Den	Ch	Binary 7654321	Hex	Den	Ch
0100001	21	33	!	1000000	40	64	@	1100000	60	96	'
0100010	22	34	"	1000001	41	65	A	1100001	61	97	a
0100011	23	35	#	1000010	42	66	B	1100010	62	98	b
0100100	24	36	$	1000011	43	67	C	1100011	63	99	c
0100101	25	37	%	1000100	44	68	D	1100100	64	100	d
0100110	26	38	&	1000101	45	69	E	1100101	65	101	e
0100111	27	39	'	1000110	46	70	F	1100110	66	102	f
0101000	28	40	(	1000111	47	71	G	1100111	67	103	g
0101001	29	41	)	1001000	48	72	H	1101000	68	104	h
0101010	2A	42	*	1001001	49	73	I	1101001	69	105	i
0101011	2B	43	+	1001010	4A	74	J	1101010	6A	106	j
0101100	2C	44	,	1001011	4B	75	K	1101011	6B	107	k
0101101	2D	45	-	1001100	4C	76	L	1101100	6C	108	l
0101110	2E	46	.	1001101	4D	77	M	1101101	6D	109	m
0101111	2F	47	/	1001110	4E	78	N	1101110	6E	110	n
0110000	30	48	0	1001111	4F	79	O	1101111	6F	111	o
0110001	31	49	1	1010000	50	80	P	1110000	70	112	p
0110010	32	50	2	1010001	51	81	Q	1110001	71	113	q
0110011	33	51	3	1010010	52	82	R	1110010	72	114	r
0110100	34	52	4	1010011	53	83	S	1110011	73	115	s
0110101	35	53	5	1010100	54	84	T	1110100	74	116	t
0110110	36	54	6	1010101	55	85	U	1110101	75	117	u
0110111	37	55	7	1010110	56	86	V	1110110	76	118	v
0111000	38	56	8	1010111	57	87	W	1110111	77	119	w
0111001	39	57	9	1011000	58	88	X	1111000	78	120	x
0111010	3A	58	:	1011001	59	89	Y	1111001	79	121	y
0111011	3B	59	;	1011010	5A	90	Z	1111010	7A	122	z
0111100	3C	60	<	1011011	5B	91	[	1111011	7B	123	{
0111101	3D	61	=	1011100	5C	92	\	1111100	7C	124		
0111110	3E	62	>	1011101	5D	93	]	1111101	7D	125	}
0111111	3F	63	?	1011110	5E	94	^	1111110	7E	126	~
				1011111	5F	95	_				

Figure 1.8   Printable ASCII characters

2 Electronic gates and registers

2.1 Logic gates

2.2 Address decoders

2.3 Three-state output devices

2.4 Sequential logic

2.5 Bus systems

2.6 Practical RAM exercise

This chapter is intended to act as a handy reference for digital electronic devices referred to in the book.

2.1 Logic gates

The two logic states required by electronic gates may be either a high and low voltage level, or a high and low current level. These may be conveniently represented by the binary digits (bits) 0 and 1. A table of binary numbers, called a truth table, may be written to describe the function of a gate or any combination of gates. Logic circuits made up of combinations of gates, where the output is directly dependent on the input at any instant, are called combinational logic circuits.

When writing down a truth table it is normal practice to write down the input combinations in numerical order. Truth tables with two alternative symbols (BS and ANSI) of the eight standard devices are shown in Section 2.1.1. The AND, OR, NAND and NOR gates are commonly available with 2, 3 or 4 inputs.

2.1.1 Gate: truth tables and symbols[1]

AND gate   The output is logic 1 only when **ALL** inputs are at logic **1**.

[1] BS   British Standards,
 ANSI   American National Standards Institute.

Input A B	Output Q
0 0	0
0 1	0
1 0	0
1 1	1

BS   ANSI

A   **&**   Q   A   Q
B   B

OR gate   The output is logic 1 when **ANY** input is at logic **1**.

Input A B	Output Q
0 0	0
0 1	1
1 0	1
1 1	1

BS   ANSI

A   **≥1**   Q   A   Q
B   B

NOT gate (**INVERTER**)   This is a single input device. The output has the opposite logic estate (complementary state) to the input.

Input A	Output Q
0	1
1	0

BS   Alternative

A   **1**   Q   A   Q

NAND gate   The output is logic 0 when **ALL** inputs are at logic **1**.

Input A B	Output Q
0 0	1
0 1	1
1 0	1
1 1	0

BS   ANSI

A   **&**   Q   A   Q
B   B

NOR gate The output is logic 0 when **ANY** input is at logic **1**.

Input A B	Output Q
0 0	1
0 1	0
1 0	0
1 1	0

Exclusive OR gate (XOR gate)   The output is logic 1 when **ONE** and only ONE input is at logic **1**.

Input A B	Output Q
0 0	0
0 1	1
1 0	1
1 1	0

Exclusive NOR gate (XNOR gate)   The output is logic 1 when **ALL** inputs are at the same logic state. This is also known as a coincidence gate.

Input A B	Output Q
0 0	1
0 1	0
1 0	0
1 1	1

Unity gain buffer amplifier   The output logic state is the same as the input.

Input A	Output Q
0	0
1	1

2.1.2   Commercial logic gates

The two commonly available families of integrated circuit logic gates (ICs) are TTL (transistor transistor logic) and CMOS (complementary metal oxide semiconductor). Both of these families have a large range of circuits which include multi-gate combinations, counters and registers. The supply and logic voltage levels are shown in Figure 2.1. TTL and CMOS ICs may be used together, but in this case CMOS ICs must be run with a 5 volt rail. It should be noted that commercial gates will accept a band of voltages for each logic state; this is important, as in a practical circuit, voltages will vary slightly due to output loading, voltage drops along connecting wires, and interference from other signals. Examples of commercial gates are shown in Section 2.1.3. Typical TTL device codes begin with 74LS and CMOS codes 40. In addition to this, some 74xx ranges, such as 74HC, are now produced using CMOS techniques. The device number follows the range identification code. Any letters before, in or after the number provide information concerning the device construction. The best place to look for further details is either the manufacturer's data book, or a supplier's catalogue.

	TTL	CMOS
Supply (rail) voltage	Vcc = 5 volts	Vdd = 5 to 15 volts
Logic 0 voltage range	0 V to 0.4 V	0 V to Vdd/2
Logic 1 voltage range	2.4 V to 5 V	Vdd/2 to Vdd

Figure 2.1   Typical commercial gate voltage levels

2.1.3   Examples of TTL and CMOS ICs

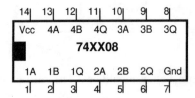

Quad 2-input AND gate

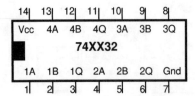

Quad 2-input OR gate

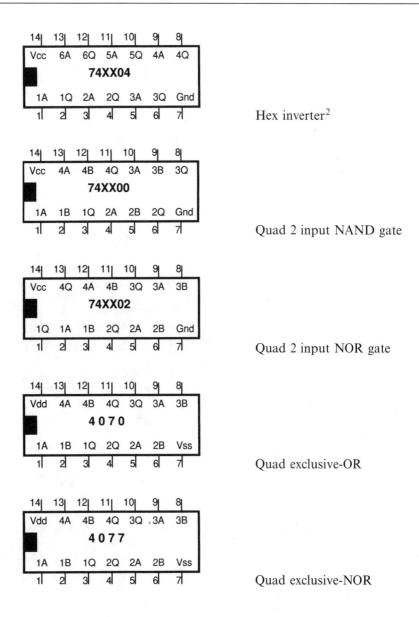

Hex inverter[2]

Quad 2 input NAND gate

Quad 2 input NOR gate

Quad exclusive-OR

Quad exclusive-NOR

2.2 Address decoders

The address decoder is an example of a combinational logic circuit. Figure 2.2 shows the truth table for a 74XX138, TTL address decoder, which selects one address from eight. An X in a truth table indicates a don't care condition.

When the correct enable signals are not supplied, all eight outputs are at logic 1. When a binary number between 000 and 111 is applied to the input, together with the correct enable signals, one of the outputs goes to logic 0.

[2] Hex is used to indicate a package of six gates; it should not be mistaken for the abbreviation for hexadecimal numbers.

Inputs						Outputs							
E0	**E1**	**E2**	**A**	**B**	**C**	**Q0**	**Q1**	**Q2**	**Q3**	**Q4**	**Q5**	**Q6**	**Q7**
1	X	X	X	X	X	1	1	1	1	1	1	1	1
X	1	X	X	X	X	1	1	1	1	1	1	1	1
X	X	0	X	X	X	1	1	1	1	1	1	1	1
0	0	1	0	0	0	0	1	1	1	1	1	1	1
0	0	1	0	0	1	1	0	1	1	1	1	1	1
0	0	1	0	1	0	1	1	0	1	1	1	1	1
0	0	1	0	1	1	1	1	1	0	1	1	1	1
0	0	1	1	0	0	1	1	1	1	0	1	1	1
0	0	1	1	0	1	1	1	1	1	1	0	1	1
0	0	1	1	1	0	1	1	1	1	1	1	0	1
0	0	1	1	1	1	1	1	1	1	1	1	1	0

Figure 2.2   Truth table of 74XX138

There are three enable inputs, E0, E1, E2. An output is only selected when E0 and E1 are at logic 0 and E2 at logic 1. Figure 2.3 shows the pinout of the 74XX138.

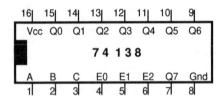

Figure 2.3   74XX138 pin assignment

2.3   Three-state output devices

In some applications, such as bus systems, it is necessary to connect outputs of gates in parallel. In these cases, to avoid bus contention[3], it is essential that only one gate produces a logic output at any instant. All the other gate outputs must be effectively switched off.

2.3.1   The three-state buffer

There are several methods of electronically disconnecting gate outputs, the most common of which is the three-state output device. The third state is known as a **high impedance** (high Z) state, it electronically disconnects the gate circuit from the output pin of the IC. This third

---

[3] Bus contention occurs if the outputs of two devices attempt to apply opposite logic states to a bus at the same time. This usually causes a high, destructive current to flow through both of the device outputs.

Data (A)	OE	Output (Q)
0	0	0
0	1	High Z
1	0	1
1	1	High Z

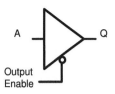

Figure 2.4 Three-state buffer, truth table and symbol

state is controlled by a signal on an *output enable* (OE) pin. Figure 2.4 shows the truth table and symbol of a three-state buffer.

A commercial, TTL *Quad, three-state, buffer* is shown in Figure 2.5.

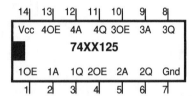

Figure 2.5 74XX125 Quad, three-state buffer

2.3.2 Static RAM input control

The logic diagram of a static RAM, Figure 2.6, shows how logic gates and three-state buffers are used to control data input/output of a *random access memory* (RAM). A '**O**' at the input terminal of a gate indicates that the signal is inverted at the gate input.

There are three control inputs which are connected to internal logic gates. The control pins are labelled output enable (OE), write enable (WE) and chip select (CS).

Referring to Figure 2.6:

CS   A **low** is required on this input to enable the memory. In a processor system this is usually connected to an output of the address decoder.

WE   To write data into memory, a **low** is required on this input. This may be supplied from the WR (write) control line of the microprocessor.

OE   A **low** on this input connects the output buffer to the data bus. The RD (read) control signal from the microprocessor may be used as an output enable signal.

A truth table of the RAM control inputs is provided in Figure 2.7.

A practical exercise, writing to and reading from a RAM, is described in Section 2.6.

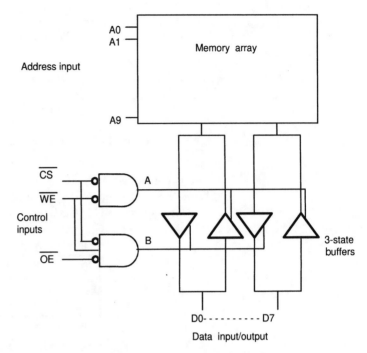

Figure 2.6   Internal control of a static RAM

Inputs CS	Inputs WE	Inputs OE	Outputs A	Outputs B	Comment
0	0	0	1	0	Data flows into RAM
0	0	1	1	0	Data flows into RAM
0	1	0	0	1	Data flows out of RAM
0	1	1	0	0	No data flow into or out of RAM
1	0	0	0	0	No data flow into or out of RAM
1	0	1	0	0	No data flow into or out of RAM
1	1	0	0	0	No data flow into or out of RAM
1	1	1	0	0	No data flow into or out of RAM

Figure 2.7   RAM control truth table

2.3.3 Octal three-state buffers

The 74XX240, Figure 2.8, is an example of a three-state inverting, 8-bit buffer. It may be used for isolating an 8-bit parallel data bus. Note that the two output enable (OE) pins are each connected to a group of four gates. The data and outputs are labelled in the conventional way, 0 to 7. Figure 2.9 is the pin assignment for this IC.

The bar over the output labels indicates that the signal is **not** the input (if data is logic 1 then the output will be logic 0 and vice versa). The bar over the OE indicates output will be enabled when a logic 0 is applied.

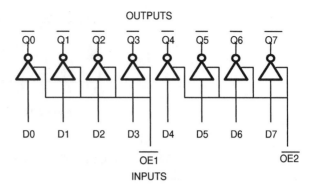

Figure 2.8 74XX240 logic diagram

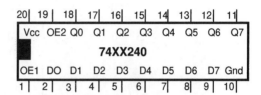

Figure 2.9 74XX240 pin assignment

2.3.4 Eight-bit bi-directional, three-state buffer

The 74XX245, illustrated in Figure 2.10 is an example of an 8-bit, *bi-directional, three-state buffer*. This is also called an octal transceiver.

This IC contains eight pairs of unity gain buffer amplifiers. It may be used to control the data direction on an 8-bit data bus. An OE pin and a data direction (DD) pin are provided.

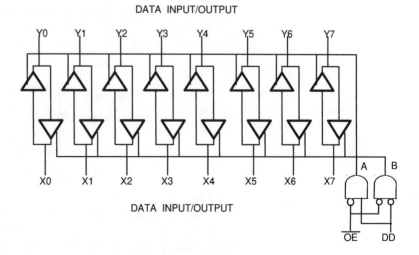

Figure 2.10 74XX245 logic diagram

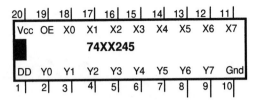

Figure 2.11 74XX245 pin assignment

The truth table Figure 2.12 shows how the output and the data direction are selected.

Inputs		Outputs		Comment
OE	DD	A	B	
0	0	0	1	Data flows from Y to X
0	1	1	0	Data flows from X to Y
1	0	0	0	Outputs inhibited
1	1	0	0	Outputs inhibited

Figure 2.12 74XX245 data direction truth table

2.4 Sequential logic

The output state of a sequential logic circuit depends upon the previous input state(s) as well as the present state.

2.4.1 The D-type latch

The D-type latch, Figure 2.13, is a basic sequential circuit. This latch circuit stores one bit of data until the application of a pulse at the clock input. The stored data is then changed if the input has changed. The input clocking pulse is sometimes called a strobe pulse.

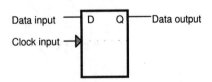

Figure 2.13 D-type latch

A timing diagram, Figure 2.14, is one means of illustrating the action of a sequential circuit. In this case, it shows that the output only changes state when the clock goes low. In some devices the *data change* takes place on the leading or trailing edge of the clock pulse.

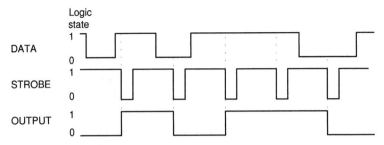

Figure 2.14 D-type latch, timing diagram

2.4.2 Octal three-state buffer, register

The logic diagram of a 74XX374, shown in Figure 2.15, contains eight D-type latches with three-state outputs. Such a device may be used to either input or output data, to or from a bus system. All the latches have a common clock input.

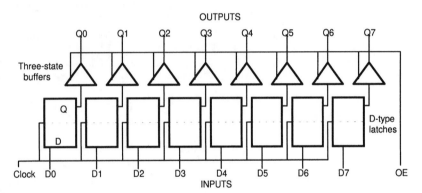

Figure 2.15 74XX374 logic diagram

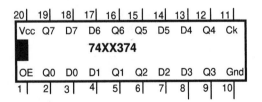

Figure 2.16 74XX374 pin assignment

2.5 Bus systems

The bus system, illustrated in Figure 2.17, provides a simple technique for connecting device inputs and outputs in parallel. Control signals are used for device selection and data transfer. Care must be taken with bus connection of device outputs to avoid bus contention. Although there are several means of achieving this, the normal method is to use three-state output devices.

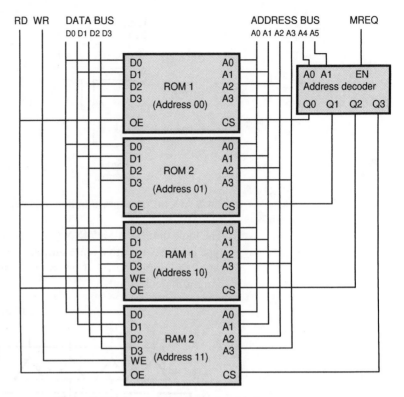

Figure 2.17   Bus connections of a simple memory system

In Figure 2.17 a 4-bit data bus and a 4-bit address bus are used to select any one of four 16-bit by 4-bit memory devices. The address decoder selects one of four devices depending on the code applied to pins A0 and A1.

The address decoder only selects a memory when the enable (EN) pin is at logic 0. Either WR or RD is at logic 0, depending on whether the memory is to input or output data. Figure 2.18 is a truth table of the address decoder.

Inputs			Outputs				Comment
EN	A1	A0	Q0	Q1	Q2	Q3	
1	0	0	1	1	1	1	No address selected
1	0	1	1	1	1	1	No address selected
1	1	0	1	1	1	1	No address selected
1	1	1	1	1	1	1	No address selected
0	0	0	0	1	1	1	ROM 1 selected
0	0	1	1	0	1	1	ROM 2 selected
0	1	0	1	1	0	1	RAM 1 selected
0	1	1	1	1	1	0	RAM 2 selected

Figure 2.18   Address decoder truth table

The total number of addresses which can be selected in Figure 2.17 is $2^6 = 64$, providing address locations from 0 to 63.

Example (a) Determine the location of data when 29_{10} is applied to the address bus of Figure 2.17.

Convert 29 to a 6-bit binary number $= 011101_{LSB}$. Thus

$$\left.\begin{array}{l} A0 = 1 \text{ LSB} \\ A1 = 0 \\ A2 = 1 \\ A3 = 1 \end{array}\right\} \text{Giving location } 1101 = 13_{10}$$

$$\left.\begin{array}{l} A4 = 1 \\ A5 = 0 \end{array}\right\} \text{In device } 01 = \text{ROM 2 (see Figure 2.18)}$$

Answer: The data is located at address 13 of ROM 2

This example shows how the higher order address lines are used to select a device whilst the lower order address lines select a location within a device. Assembly language programming, requires the programmer to know the range of addresses available, but the actual selection of the memory chip is normally transparent.

2.6 Practical RAM exercise

The aim of this exercise, which uses a 2K by 8-bit RAM, is to write into 16 locations of memory the bit patterns for a 7-segment indicator to produce displays from 0 to F. Unused memory address connections must be grounded otherwise the location of data in the memory will be uncertain. The wiring diagram is given in Figure 2.19, and the first few lines of the 7-segment code are provided in Figure 2.20.

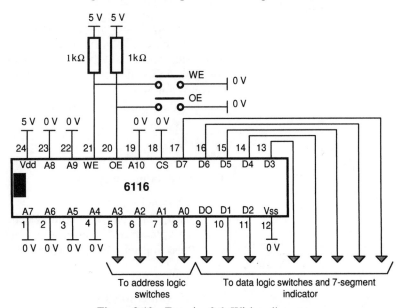

Figure 2.19 Exercise 2.6: Wiring diagram

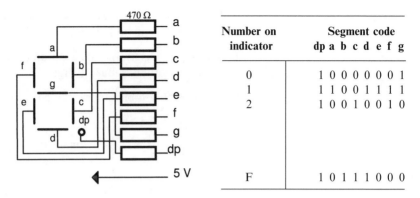

Number on indicator	Segment code dp a b c d e f g
0	1 0 0 0 0 0 0 1
1	1 1 0 0 1 1 1 1
2	1 0 0 1 0 0 1 0
F	1 0 1 1 1 0 0 0

Figure 2.20   Exercise 2.6: 7-segment information

Items required:

Quantity Y	Item	Comment
1	6118 RAM	2K RAM
1	Proto-board	For circuit assembly
2	1 kΩ	Switch pull-up resistors
1	7-segment ind.	A common anode device is used in this description
1	DIL 8 × 470 Ω	Current limiting resistors for the 7-segment indicator
2	Press switches	Output enable and write enable switches
2	Switch boxes	These are described in Chapter 14, but any logic switches may be used

Part of the binary code for a common anode, 7-segment indicator is shown in Figure 2.20, pin connections depend on the type of indicator used (they can usually be obtained from the supplier's catalogue). With common anode devices a logic 0 applied to a segment switches it on. Current limiting resistors, connected between the segments and the memory data pins, will be required.

Operation

To write data into memory

1   **OE** switch open
2   Set up data on data input switches
3   Set up address on address switches
4   Press and release **WE** switch.

To read data

1   **OE** switch to closed
2   Select address on address input switches.

3 An 8-bit microprocessor

3.1 Introduction to microprocessors

3.2 An 8-bit microprocessor system

3.3 The Zilog Z80 CPU

Chapters 3, 4 and 5 provide the basis for an investigation of micro-processor-based systems. The intention in this chapter is to review the essential elements of an 8-bit microprocessor system. The material is mainly included for completeness, and should be familiar ground to those who have already studied microprocessor systems.

3.1 Introduction to microprocessors

A microprocessor system has two distinct, but interdependent, parts, *software* and *hardware*, see Figure 3.1. Neither part can function without the other. Programs stored on ROM may be referred to as firmware. A program consists of a sequence of MPU instructions which have been stored in memory. The MPU operates by *fetching* and *executing* these instructions. It controls all data transfers, and carries out arithmetic and logic operations.

Each type[1] of MPU has its own set of machine code instructions. These may range from 1 to 5 bytes of binary code, see Section 3.3.4. Instructions, combined to produce a *program*, may initially be written in either *low level*[2] assembly language or in a *high level*[3] language such as C or Pascal. Normally a text editor and assembler are used for low level language programming. The assembler should produce a ⟨*name*⟩.*com* file, which simply contains machine code. The assembler may also produce a ⟨*name*⟩.*hex* file which contains the machine code written in ASCII, and a ⟨*name*⟩.*lst* file which contains both the original program and the machine code.

[1] In this case 'type' may mean a family of MPUs developed by the same manufacturer.

[2] Low level language: each type or family of MPU(s) has its own assembly language which consists of the symbolic or mnemonic representation of instructions such as *ld a, b*.

[3] High level languages are used for writing programs for any MPU, for which a suitable compiler is available, see Chapter 7.

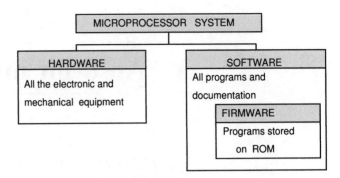

Figure 3.1   Components of a microprocessor system

3.2 An 8-bit microprocessor system

The logic circuit of a basic microprocessor system is shown in Figure 3.2. The *hardware* comprises an MPU, an address decoder, a read only memory (ROM), a random access memory (RAM) and parallel input and output registers.

3.2.1 System operation

The input/output registers interface the system to peripheral equipment. They allow 8-bit data words to be transferred to and from the system respectively, to devices such as a printer, keypad, or LED displays.

The sequence of 8-bit instructions[4], previously stored in memory, are read into the MPU on the data bus. Instructions may be made up of from 1 to 5 bytes. The rate at which instructions are processed is controlled by the *clock* frequency. Five to 20 MHz are typical clock frequencies for 8-bit machines.

3.2.2 The microprocessor unit (MPU)

The MPU is described in detail in Section 3.3, so only the basic operation is covered here. Following a *reset* the address of the first instruction is applied to the address bus, MREQ and RD are then asserted. The processor will now *fetch* a byte of instruction from memory via the data bus. The instruction is *decoded* and a sequence of control signals subsequently generated to control both internal and external operations. If additional data is required, in order to complete the instruction, it will be fetched from memory. Finally the instruction is *executed*. This process continues until either a **halt** or a loop instruction is executed by the MPU.

[4] See Section 3.3.4 for processor instructions.

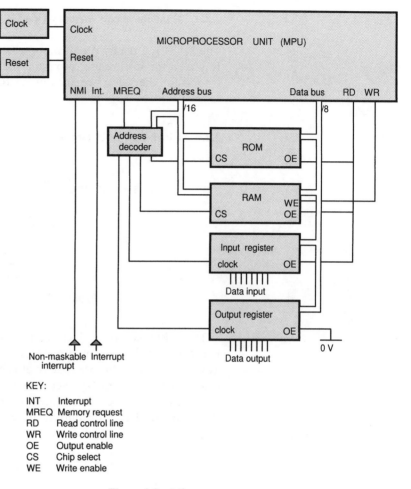

Figure 3.2   Microprocessor system

3.2.3   Read only memory (ROM)

Firmware, stored in the ROM, which is a non-volatile[5] device, will be in the machine code[6] of the MPU being used. This will contain the initialization program, and any other permanent information required by the processor. The ROM stores the start-up program called a bootstrap, or monitor program to initialize the system. Alternatively, in a dedicated[7] system it may contain the entire program.

---

[5] The contents of a non-volatile memory are not lost when the system is switched off.

[6] Machine code is the set of MPU instructions in binary code, usually written in hexadecimal form. For example, the machine code for load A with the contents of B (**ld a, b**) is 78H.

[7] A dedicated system is one which is designed to perform specific functions.

3.2.4   Random access memory (RAM)

The RAM is a read/write memory which may be volatile or non-volatile. It is used for storing user programs and data. A small part of the RAM is used for the *stack*, see Section 3.2.10.

3.2.5   Clock and reset circuits

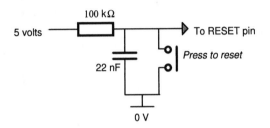

Figure 3.3   Auto/Manual reset

The MPU requires a clock input to synchronize the system. The clock is a 0 to 5 volt constant frequency rectangular wave. Single chips are available for this purpose. The reset is normally held at logic 1. A logic 0 causes the system to be reset. Figure 3.3 shows the CR circuit which automatically causes the processor to go to its start address when switched on. The *reset* button allows the processor to be reset to its start address at any time.

3.2.6   Address bus

The *address bus* consists of 16 conductors labelled A0 to A15. It carries addresses generated by the MPU. The address specifies the source, or destination, of data which will transit along the *data bus*. With 16 address lines it is possible to address 2^{16} ($= 65536$) locations (64K in computing terms).

3.2.7   Data bus

The *bi-directional data bus* has eight conductors, labelled D0 to D7. This bus allows data transfer, either from the MPU to any other system component, or from one of the system components to the MPU. A data transfer timing diagram is shown in Figure 3.10.

3.2.8 The control bus

The control bus consists of a number of conductors, some of which carry signals into the MPU and others carry signals from the MPU. Seven control conductors are shown in Figure 3.2, MREQ, RD, WR are signals from the MPU, and Reset, Clock, NMI and Int., are signals into the MPU. A logic 0 on an interrupt (Int. or NMI) pin, normally held at logic 1, causes the MPU to suspend execution of the current program and execute an interrupt routine, see Section 3.3.7.

3.2.9 Address decoder

All the devices in this system are memory mapped, which means that they are selected by the address decoder, according to the memory map of Figure 3.4. The decoder selects one of the four devices from address lines A14 and A15. These lines are connected to the address decoder input so that the ROM is selected by 00, the RAM by 01, the input by 10 and the output by 11, see Figure 3.5.

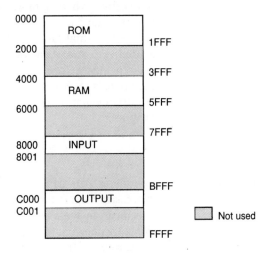

Figure 3.4 Memory map

3.2.10 The stack

The stack is a form of note pad for the microprocessor. It is used automatically to store return addresses when:

(i) Executing **call** and **rst** instructions.
(ii) Processing interrupts.

The contents of registers used in subroutines may be copied to the stack

Address lines	15	14	13	12	11	10	9	8	7	6	5	4	3	2	1	0
ROM first	0	0	0	0	0	0	0	0	0	0	0	0	0	0	0	0
Addresses last	0	0	0	1	1	1	1	1	1	1	1	1	1	1	1	1
RAM first	0	1	0	0	0	0	0	0	0	0	0	0	0	0	0	0
Addresses last	0	1	0	1	1	1	1	1	1	1	1	1	1	1	1	1
INPUT Reg.	1	0	0	0	0	0	0	0	0	0	0	0	0	0	0	0
OUTPUT Reg.	1	1	0	0	0	0	0	0	0	0	0	0	0	0	0	0
Decoder inputs																

Figure 3.5   Address line selector

using the **push** instruction and retrieved from the stack with the **pop** (or **pull**) instruction.

A stack is a designated block of RAM in which data is stored and retrieved on a last in first out (LIFO) basis. The stack pointer stores the last address where data was stored on the stack. It should be initialized at an early stage in the program.

The top (highest address) of the stack is fixed by a 16-bit address, loaded into the stack pointer (SP) register, see Figure 3.7. The SP is decremented before each byte is pushed to the stack and incremented as each byte is retrieved from the stack. See Section 3.3.6 for a programming example which demonstrates the stack operation for a segment of Z80 program.

3.3   The Zilog Z80 CPU

The Zilog Z80 CPU is used in this section as an example of an 8-bit processor. Significant points are included from the Zilog Products Specification Data Book and the information is reproduced by permission of Zilog, Inc. Copyright 1989, 1991, 1994 and 1995.

Features of this microprocessor, referred to in the Zilog manual as the Z80 CPU (central processing unit) include:

(i)   NMOS[8] version for low cost, high performance solutions. Clock frequencies of 4 MHz and 6.17 MHz.
(ii) CMOS[9] version for high performance, low power designs. Clock frequencies up to 20 MHz.
(iii) Duplicate set of both general-purpose and flag registers, which, used with 'exchange' instructions, provide for foreground/background mode or very fast interrupt response.
(iv) Two 16-bit index registers.

[8] NMOS   N-channel metal-oxide-semiconductor.
[9] CMOS   Complementary MOS (uses both n-channel and p-channel devices).

(v) Three modes of maskable interrupt. Mode 0, 1 and 2 as described in Section 3.3.7.

3.3.1 General description

The internal block diagram of Figure 3.6 shows the primary functions of the CPU. All instruction input, and data input/output, are via the data bus. Data is written to, or received from, an address output by the MPU on the address bus. The CPU has three main elements:

(i) Control: instructions are entered into the instruction register, decoded and then initiate control signals from the CPU timing and control block.
(ii) Arithmetic and logic operations.
(iii) General-purpose and designated registers, see Figure 3.7.

Arithmetic and logic operations are executed by the accumulator (A), the arithmetic and logic unit (ALU), and the status register (F). The ALU is a combinational logic unit which performs *both arithmetic* and *logic* functions

Instructions such as shift and rotate are executed in the accumulator. The *result* of operations like **add** and **sub**tract are placed in the accumulator. The status register records the results of certain operations as described in Section 3.3.2.

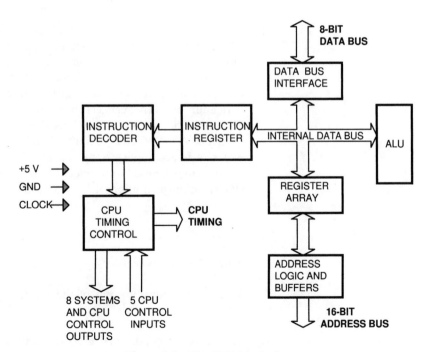

Figure 3.6 Z80 CPU block diagram

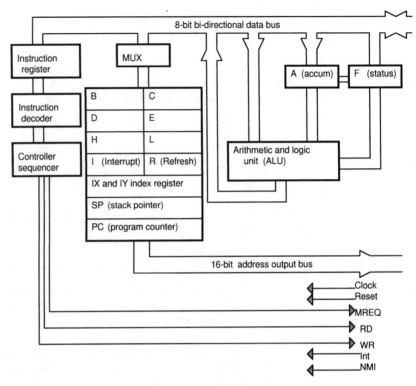

Figure 3.7   Internal MPU organisation

Registers are selected by the multiplexer (MUX). The six 8-bit registers (B, C, D, E, H, L) may be used in programs singularly or in pairs as 16-bit registers. Some registers have special instructions; for instance B is used as a loop counter and HL may be used as an address pointer. There are also two special-purpose registers (interrupt) I and (refresh) R.

In addition to the registers shown in Figure 3.7, registers A, B, C, D, E, H, L and F are all duplicated. This alternative register set is designated by ($'$), hence A$'$, B$'$, C$'$, D$'$, E$'$, H$'$, L$'$ and F$'$. Transfer of data between the two sets is accomplished by the use of 'exchange' instructions. These registers may be used to provide a faster response to interrupts, and easy, efficient implementation of background–foreground techniques.

3.3.2   The status register

Two of the main purposes of the status register (register F, Figure 3.7) are to:

(i)   Facilitate conditional **jump** and **call** instructions such as **jp nz,start** (jump, if zero-flag-not-set, to start).

(ii) Detect overflow errors caused by 2's complement calculations. These can occur when adding two large numbers of the same sign, or subtracting two large numbers of different signs.

Figure 3.8 shows the functions of the status register bits. Each bit is set or reset during the execution of instructions, such as **add**, **sub**tract, **comp**are, to indicate if the result is positive, negative, zero, carry, half-carry or overflow.

Logic 0 indicates that a flag is **not set** or **cleared**
Logic 1 indicates that a flag is **set**.

Status register	S	Z		H		P/V	N	C
Bit	7	6	5	4	3	2	1	0

Bit	Bit label	Comment
7	Sign	Set if negative, Clear if positive
6	Zero	Set if zero, Clear if NOT zero
4	Half carry	Set if there is a carry from first 4 bits, else Clear
2	Overflow	Set if 2's complement overflow occurs, else Clear
1	Add/Subtract	Set for subtract, Clear for add
0	Carry	Set if there is a carry, else Clear
5&3		Internal use

Figure 3.8   The status (F) register

Example (a)   Status flags.

The table in Figure 3.9 shows the result of executing the instruction **add a,n**:

Which causes the contents of the accumulator (register A) to be added to the contents of the memory location immediately following the opcode. The result is stored in the accumulator.

The opcode for **add a,n** is 11000110 (C6 hex)

MC code	Number in accumulator	Number n	Result in accumulator	S	Z	H	V	N	C
C6 00	0000 0000	0000 0000	0000 0000	0	1	0	0	0	0
C6 00	0001 0000	0000 0000	0001 0000	0	0	0	0	0	0
C6 01	0001 1111	0000 0001	0010 0000	0	0	1	0	0	0
C6 01	1111 1111	0000 0001	0000 0000	0	1	1	0	0	1
C6 90	1000 0000	1001 0000	0001 0000	0	0	0	1	0	1
C6 70	1000 0000	0111 0000	1111 0000	1	0	0	0	0	0
C6 70	0111 0000	0111 0000	1110 0000	1	0	0	1	0	0

Figure 3.9   add a,n results

The left-hand column of Figure 3.9 shows the machine code in hexadecimal, opcode first followed by number **n**.

3.3.3   MPU timing diagram

One method of showing the relationship of the control, address bus and data bus is a timing diagram as shown in Figure 3.10. The CPU has several different timing sequences according to the operation it is performing. In Figure 3.10 a typical memory read/write cycle is shown. Both the read and the write take three clock periods (a total period of 150 ns for each operation, when using a 20 MHz clock).

With reference to the numbers on Figure 3.10:

1 The address of the memory location to be accessed is placed on the address bus.
2 One half clock period later, MREQ and RD are asserted.
3 MPU reads data on the falling edge of the T3 clock.
4 MREQ and RD released (back to logic 1).
5 Memory address is removed from address bus.
6 The memory location where data is to be written is placed on the address bus.
7 One half clock period later, when the address has had time to settle, MREQ is asserted. This can be used as a chip enable for memory devices.
8 The MPU places data to be written to memory on the data bus.

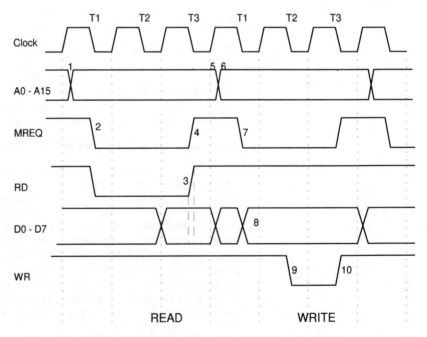

Figure 3.10   Memory read/write timing diagram

9 When the data bus has had time to settle, WR is asserted and so provides a read/write signal for memory chips.

10 WR and MREQ are released a half clock period before information on the address or data bus is altered.

3.3.4 Instructions and addressing modes

The Z80 has one of the most powerful and versatile instruction sets available in any 8-bit MPU. It includes such unique operations as a block move, for fast, efficient data transfers within memory, or between memory and I/O. It also allows operations on any bit in any location in memory.

Each machine code instruction has its own code known as an *opcode*. Additional information may be required to implement an instruction. This additional information, called operands, may be included as part of the opcode byte, or it may be contained in 1 or more additional bytes which follow the opcode. Hence the opcode specifies the operation to be performed on operands which are either stored in MPU registers or external memory.

The addressing mode specifies how the operand is actually referenced. Different addressing modes are provided to:

(i) Give programming versatility to the user, providing such facilities as pointers to memory, counters for loop control, indexing of data, and program relocation.

(ii) Reduce the number of bits in the addressing field of the instruction.

The main addressing modes used in 8-bit systems are:

(i) Implicit (implied) (register)
   ld a,b   copy contents of register B into A
(ii) Immediate load register A with an 8-bit number
   ld a,n
(iii) Absolute   jump to a 16-bit address
   jp nn
(iv) Relative   relative jump forwards up to 129 addresses, or back to
   jr n   126 addresses
(v) Direct   copy contents of memory location nn to register A
   ld a,(nn)
(vi) Indirect   copy the contents of memory location stored in BC to
   ld a,(bc) register A

n = an 8-bit number, nn = a 16-bit address.

3.3.5 Addressing mode examples

Implicit, implied or register mode   Instructions which operate exclusively on registers normally use implicit, also known as implied, or register mode. Instructions such as complement accumulator need no further information as it is implied that the operand is in the accumulator.

Example (b)   Complement accumulator

cpl   Machine Code: 2F
If the accumulator contains   3DH = 0011 1101
After execution   C2H = 1100 0010

Immediate   In this mode the opcode is followed by a 1- or a 2-byte operand.

Example (c)

ld a, 5B   Machine code 3E 5B   Load register A with
                                              number 5BH

ld bc,4131   Machine code 01 31 41   Load register B with 41
                                              and register C with 31

Example (d)

jp 3025   Machine code C3 25 30   Overwrite PC contents
                                              with 3025.

Direct (absolute)   The opcode, which may be 1 or 2 bytes, is followed by 2 bytes giving the address where the operand is to be stored, or where it is to be retrieved from.

Example (e)

ld (040BH),bc   Machine code ED 43 0B 04   The contents of registers
                                               BC are to be stored at
                                               memory address 040BH.

Indirect   The address of the operand has been previously loaded into a register pair. Hence this instruction can be a single byte of opcode.

Example (f)

ld a,(bc)   Machine code: 0A   Data 5CH is in memory at
                                               address 3B45H. 3B45H
                                               has been loaded into
                                               registers BC. After
                                               execution A contains
                                               5CH

Relative   In an 8-bit system relative addressing has a 2-byte format, and so provides more efficient branching than absolute addressing. The branch opcode byte is followed by a byte of relative address which counts either forwards 127 locations or backwards 128 locations from the number in the PC (the address of the next instruction).

Example (g)   The address of the following instruction is 1000H.

jr 12H   Machine code: 18 12   Before fetch   PC = 1000
                                           After fetch   PC = 1002
                                           After execution   PC = 1014.

Example (h)   The address of the following instruction is 1000H.

jr -20H[10]   Machine code: 18 E0   Before fetch   PC = 1000
                                           After fetch   PC = 1002
                                           After execution   PC = 0FE2[11].

3.3.6   The program

The following ⟨*name.lst*⟩ file of a short assembly language program
shows the operation of the stack pointer and the program counter. The
pseudo[12] instruction 'org' indicates the start address of the program, and
'equ' attaches addresses to labels[13].

To execute the **call** instruction, the MPU has first to **push** the contents
of the program counter (PC) to the stack. The PC contents are restored
after execution of the subroutine.

The description of the **djnz n** instruction used in the program is:

Subtract 1 from the number in the B register. If the result is NOT zero
(if the zero flag is not set as a result of this subtraction) add the byte
stored at the next address to the number in the program counter using
2's complement arithmetic.

In the example program, the machine code at address 0308H is 10 FB.

10 is the **djnz n** instruction
FB is the number to be added to the PC to go to address of LOOP.

The PC contents at this point is 030AH, as the PC always holds the
address of the next instruction. Note FBH is sign extended[14] for the
addition.

---

[10] The 2's complement of 20H is E0H, see Chapter 1.

[11] 2's complement addition   1002 = 0001 0000 0000 0010
$$+E0 = \underline{1111\ 1111\ 1110\ 0000}$$
$$0000\ 1111\ 1110\ 0010 = 0FE2H$$

[12] Pseudo instructions are used to give the assembler information, they are not
part of the MPU manufacturer's assembly language. Different assembler writers
may use slightly different instructions.

[13] When writing programs it is generally better to use relevant labels for any
addresses and constants appearing in the program. This makes the program more
readable and it is much easier to modify the program to run on machines with a
different memory map.

[14] Sign extension means that if bit 7 of, say, an 8-bit number is 0, then to convert
to a 16-bit number, fill bits 8 to 15 with 0s. Similarly if bit 7 of an 8-bit number is 1
then fill bits 8 to 15 with 1s.

Hence

$$0000\ 0011\ 0000\ 1010$$
$$+\ \underline{1111\ 1111\ 1111\ 1011}$$
$$\overline{0000\ 0011\ 0000\ 0101} = 0305\text{H new PC contents}$$

Example (i)   CALLing a subroutine.

The following *listing file* in Figure 3.11 is a sample program showing how a subroutine is called from a main program. A trace table showing stack operations is provided in Figure 3.12.

Assembly language and machine code program				
	org	100H		;start address of program
stack	equ	600H		;initialise stack pointer
screen	equ	0FF0CH[15]		;Screen output routine
;- -				
;Address	Machine Code	Label	Instruction	Comment
0100	31 00 06		ld sp, stack	;load stack pointer
0103	01 78 56		ld bc, 5678H	;load bc with number
0106	CD 00 03	start:	call subrtn	;call subroutine
0109	{next Instruction}			
;- -				
0300	C5	subrtn:	push bc	;save contents of BC
0301	06 02		ld b,02	;load B with 2
0303	0E 2A		ld c, '*'	;load C with ASCII 2A
0305	CD 0C FF	loop:	call screen	;print *
0308	10 FB		djnz loop	;B-1 if B NOT 0,loop
030A	C1		pop bc	;restore contents BC
030B	C9		ret	;return to main program.

Figure 3.11   Listing file of program sample

It is important to remember that all instructions and data are stored in binary code as illustrated in Figure 3.13.

The **call** instruction requires five external memory operations. It takes a total of 17 clock cycles. If the clock frequency is 20 MHz the total time is 850 ns. This time may be compared with the Intel 32-bit, 80386 MPU, which typically takes 12 clock cycles to execute a **call** instruction. With a clock frequency of 33 MHz this processor takes $12/33 \times 10^6 \ (= 363.6\,\text{ns})$, about two and a half times quicker than the Z80.

3.3.7   Interrupts

The versatility of a microprocessor is enhanced by the provision of hardware interrupt facilities. These provide for the possibility of a

---

[15] Some assemblers require a 0 in front of hexadecimal numbers which begin with a letter symbol, to indicate that it is a number and not a label.

Instruction		BC	PC next address	SP	Stack data
ld sp, stack			0103	0600	
ld bc, 5678H		56 78	0106		
call subrtn	(high byte)			05FF	01
	(low byte)		0300	05FE	09
push bc				05FD	78
			0301	05FC	56
ld b, 02		02 78	0303		
ld c, 2AH		02 2A	0305		
call screen				05FB	03
	(Print*)		FF0C	05FA	08
djnz loop			0308	05FC	56
		01 2A	0305		
call screen				05FB	03
	(Print*)		FF0C	05FA	08
djnz loop			0308	05FC	56
		00 2A	030A		
pop bc		56 78	030B	05FE	01
ret			1009	0600	

Figure 3.12   Trace table for Example (i)

Main program		Subroutine	
Address	**Data**	**Address**	**Data**
0000 0001 0000 0000	0011 0001	0000 0011 0000 0000	1100 0101
0000 0001 0000 0001	0000 0000	0000 0011 0000 0001	0000 0110
0000 0001 0000 0010	0000 0110	0000 0011 0000 0010	0000 0010
0000 0001 0000 0011	0000 0001	0000 0011 0000 0011	0000 1110
0000 0001 0000 0100	0111 1000	0000 0011 0000 0100	0010 1010
0000 0001 0000 0101	0101 0110	0000 0011 0000 0101	1100 1101
0000 0001 0000 0110	1100 1101	0000 0011 0000 0110	0000 1100
0000 0001 0000 0111	0000 0000	0000 0011 0000 0111	1111 1111
0000 0001 0000 1000	0000 0011	0000 0011 0000 1000	0001 0000
0000 0001 0000 1001		0000 0011 0000 1001	1111 1011
		0000 0011 0000 1010	1100 0001
		0000 0011 0000 1011	1100 1001

Figure 3.13   Trace table for Example (i)

processor system doing several tasks virtually at the same time, such as processing data and servicing peripherals.

An MPU may have several interrupt pins, in the case of the Z80 there is an INT pin and an NMI pin. A logic 0 on one of these pins may interrupt the processing at any time. An interrupt will generally cause the execution of the current program to be suspended, a service routine executed, and then return to the current program. In addition to the interrupt mechanisms, the external buses of a Z80 system may be controlled by applying a logic 0 to the bus BUSRQ (bus request) pin.

Bus request   When the BUSRQ is asserted the MPU suspends current operations, and sets both the data and the address bus to the high impedance state. Control signals which are not three-state are placed into the non-asserted state. Handshaking is provided by the Z80 outputting a logic 0 on the BUSAK (bus acknowledge) pin. This facility is mainly used for direct memory access (DMA). That is, the transfer of data directly between a peripheral and the microprocessor system memory.

NMI (non-maskable interrupt)   As the name implies this interrupt cannot be inhibited. It will be accepted by the MPU on completion of the current program instruction. If an NMI is received during a BUSRQ it will be serviced when the BUSRQ is finished.

The NMI causes the PC contents to be pushed to stack and then loads address 0066H into the PC. Either a jump or a service routine must be written starting at 0066H. At the end of the service routine the instruction **retn** must be used to return from non-maskable interrupt.

Int (interrupt)   This interrupt is enabled by the program instruction **ei** and disabled with the instruction **di**. There are three modes of operation, 0, 1 and 2, which are selected by using instructions **im 0**, **im 1** or **im 2** respectively. Interrupt routines using this mode must end with the instruction **reti**. Instruction **ei** must appear in the interrupt routine before **reti**, see Examples (k) and (l).

Interrupt mode 0   The Z80 operates in this mode after reset or after the **im 0** instruction has been executed. The MPU expects either an **rst** or a **call** instruction to be placed on the data bus. Both of these instructions cause the PC contents to be *pushed* to the stack and then branch to an address. **rst** is a 1-byte instruction which provides for a jump to one of eight addresses (00H, 08H, 10H, 18H, 20H, 28H, 30H, 38H).

Interrupt mode 1   This mode is set by executing the **im 1** instruction. It operates the same as NMI except that the branch is to location 0038H.

Interrupt mode 2 (vectored interrupts)   This mode is set by executing an **im 2** instruction. The interrupt vector is an address supplied by the peripheral device which generated the interrupt. It is used as the lower byte of a memory pointer to the start address of the interrupt handling routine.

Indirect addressing is used. The 16-bit address of the interrupt routine is made up as follows:

A0 > 0 (must be zero for 2-byte address)
A1 to A7 from the peripheral is placed on the data lines
A8 to A15 from the I register (which has been previously loaded with the upper byte of the interrupt vector table address).

The table may contain up to 128 16-bit addresses where interrupt handling routines are stored. This provides for 128 peripherals to select their own routine by applying a 7-bit address to a parallel input port.

Example (j) Vectored addressing.

Interrupt vector table start address is 8000H, so 80H is loaded into the MPU I-register. There are four devices in the system, which provide vector values of 00, 02, 04, 06.

The interrupt handler information is shown in Figure 3.14, and the vector table in Figure 3.15 A system diagram showing values when device 2 has caused the interrupt is shown in Figure 3.16.

Device number	Vector	Handler address
1	00	A000
2	02	A050
3	04	A07F
4	06	A0A2

Figure 3.14 Interrupt information

Address	Handler address
80 00	00
80 01	A0
80 02	50
80 03	A0
80 04	7F
80 05	A0
80 06	A2
80 07	A0

Figure 3.15 Interrupt vector table stored in memory

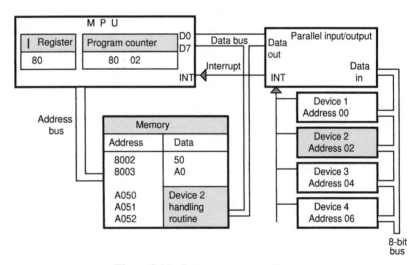

Figure 3.16 Interrupt system diagram

3.3.8 Short interrupt routine

The contents of any registers used in interrupt routines must first be **push**ed to stack and **pop**ped in the reverse order at the end of the routine. Blank stubs for a non-maskable and a maskable mode 1 interrupt routine are shown below, followed by a main program start-up routine.

Example (k)   Non-maskable interrupt routine.

Address   Machine code   Assembler   Comment

0066	f5	push af	;only push registers used in
0067	c5	push bc	;the routine
0068	d5	push de	
{ routine }			
0080	d1	pop de	
0081	c1	pop bc	
0082	f1	pop af	
0083	ed 45	retn	;return from non maskable interrupt

Example (l)   Interrupt routine mode 1.

Address   Machine code   Assembler   Comment

0038	f5	push af	
0039	c5	push bc	
003A	d5	push de	
{ routine }			
0050	d1	pop de	
0051	c1	pop bc	
0052	f1	pop af	
0053	fb	ei	;enable interrupt again
0054	ed 4d	reti	;return from interrupt

Example (m)   Main program start-up routine.

The Z80 goes to address 0000 after reset. Programs are assumed to start at address 0100. The memory map of Figure 3.4 has been used.

Address   Machine code   Assembler   Comment

0000	31 FF 5F	ld sp,5FFFH	;initialise stack pointer
0003	ed 56	im 1	;initialise interrupt mode 1
0005	fb	ei	;enable interrupt
0006	c3 00 01	jp 0100H	;jump to address where main
0100			;program starts

Part Two
Theory and Programming

4 Types of microprocessor

4.1 Types of microprocessor

4.2 MPU techniques

4.3 Complex instruction set computer (CISC)

4.4 Reduced instruction set computer (RISC)

4.5 Single chip microcontrollers

The main aim of this chapter is to look at three different approaches to microprocessor design, CISC, RISC and single chip. Figure 4.1 illustrates the relationship between these three divisions.

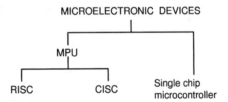

Figure 4.1   Microelectronic device tree

4.1 Types of microprocessor

RISC and CISC are two alternative design approaches. The main features of CISC design are listed in Section 4.3 and those of RISC in Section 4.4.

Systems in which microprocessors are incorporated may be described as:

(i)   Stand-alone.
(ii) Dedicated.
(iii) Embedded.

A typical example of a *stand-alone* system is the personal computer (PC), described in Chapter 5.

The *single chip microcontroller*, Section 4.5, is especially useful for *dedicated* systems which are designed for specific applications such as printer control, airflow measurements or automatic baud rate detection.

An *embedded* system is where the microprocessor forms part of another system, such as a car engine, an aircraft or a weapons system. With such systems tight control of processor execution time is usually necessary. This can be achieved by using assembly language or alternatively the high level language called ADA, which was especially developed for this purpose.

4.1.1   Aims of a system design

The system design will be influenced by whether cost or speed is the main criterion. When comparing microprocessor systems, factors which should be considered are:

(i)   Speed of processing and data transfer.
(ii) Cost of the system.
(iii) Input/Output facilities.
(iv) Physical size.

4.1.2   Speed of processing and data transfer

Items which influence the speed of processing:

(i)   The clock frequency supplied to the MPU.
(ii) The width of the system data bus.
(iii) The MPU instruction execution time.
(iv) The design of the system.
(v)   Software design and programming techniques.

There is inevitably constant development to improve the speed at which microprocessor systems operate. Clearly the faster the system, the faster and more detailed the results presented to the system user.

The clock frequency of desktop computers, which directly controls the rate of processing, has increased by about 100 times in the past decade. The system designer has limited control of the clock frequency, in that a range of frequencies is usually specified for a particular MPU by the manufacturer.

In recent years the width of the data bus has increased from 8 bits to 16 bits and then to 32 bits. With a wider data bus there are relatively fewer references to memory, thus reducing memory access time.

The MPU instruction execution time, together with the clock frequency and the bus widths, are determined by the MPU selected for the system. Techniques used by MPU manufacturers to reduce execution times are described in Section 4.2.

The program design and the programming techniques used can determine the ultimate speed of the system. For example, the program should be designed so that the processor does not have to perform unnecessary calculations during the execution of the program. The code should be optimised so that the most efficient instructions are used for executing a particular function.

4.1.3   Cost of the system

The following items will influence the cost of a processor system:

 (i) Cost of components.
 (ii) Number of ICs.
 (iii) Width of address bus.
 (iv) Width of data bus.
 (v) Type of memory.

The cost of the individual components of a processor system will clearly depend on the market price at the time the system is produced. In general, recently developed devices will cost more than devices which have been in service for some years.

   The number of ICs (the chip count) in a system will influence the cost in several ways: in addition to the purchase of the ICs, circuit board size, chip connections and testing must be taken into account. From this point of view the single chip microcontroller (Section 4.5) has an advantage over the microprocessor systems. Generally speaking, the wider the address and data buses, the more expensive the system. If the full memory addressing capability of the MPU is not required, the width of the address bus may be reduced. However, possible future development of the system must be kept in mind. If cost reduction is more important than system speed, a processor which will operate with a data bus half the width of the data output could be selected, i.e. a 16-bit processor may be used in a system with an 8-bit data bus.

   Memory chips with shorter access times are generally more expensive, thus increasing the cost of faster systems.

4.1.4   Input/Output facilities

MPUs normally have two types of input facilities, a parallel data bus and interrupt. The only output from the MPU is the parallel data bus. All other I/O facilities must be part of the system design and may include both parallel and serial ports. The single chip microcontroller, on the other hand, will have parallel, serial and possibly analogue I/O.

4.1.5   Physical size

The physical size of the package will to a large extent be determined by the number of pins required. These again will depend on the bus widths. The number of connections required will be the sum of the address bus, data bus and control bus plus the supply connections. On some chips connections are multiplexed giving pins more than one function.

4.2   MPU techniques

In this section a number of techniques are described which may be used to improve MPU performance. The descriptions are intended to show the principle of the idea. The implementation will generally be much more sophisticated.

Performance improving techniques described are:

(i)   Pipelining, Section 4.2.1.
(ii)   Cache memory, Section 4.2.2.
(iii)   Overlapped window registers, Section 4.2.3.
(iv)   MPU timing and control, Section 4.2.4.

4.2.1   Pipelining

Pipelining is a means of increasing the processing rate by dividing a task into a number of segments, and then processing the segments in parallel. Each segment, normally consisting of a combinational logic circuit, is separated by a register. Pipelining is typically applied to instructions and arithmetic operations. An arithmetic pipeline is demonstrated in Example (b).

An instruction pipeline reads consecutive instructions from memory, while previously read instructions are being processed in other segments. This causes the instruction *fetch* and *execute* phases to overlap and so gives the possibility of executing an instruction per clock cycle, see Example (a).

Example (a)   Instruction pipelining.

Figure 4.2 shows an instruction pipeline which has five segments. If each segment takes a period of one clock cycle then the processor is virtually working at one instruction per clock cycle.

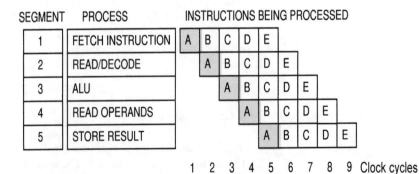

Figure 4.2   Using a 5-segment pipeline for processing five instructions A, B, C, D and E

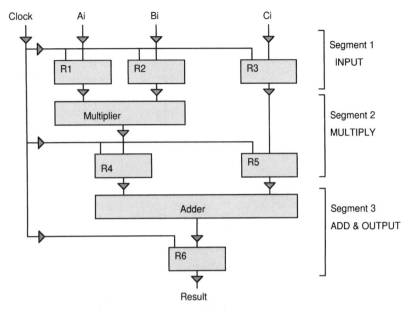

Figure 4.3 Pipeline arithmetic processing

Example (b) Arithmetic pipelining.

This example illustrates a 3-segment pipelining system, using registers and combinational logic, for calculating:

$$Ai * Bi + Ci \quad \text{for } i = 1, 2, 3, \ldots, 9$$

Figure 4.3 shows how the operations are divided into three segments. The result of each segment calculation is stored in a register, and then clocked to the next segment. The suboperations are:

Segment 1 (Input)	$Ai \rightarrow R1$,	$Bi \rightarrow R2$,	$Ci \rightarrow R3$
Segment 2 (Multiply)	$R1 * R2 \rightarrow R4$,	$R3 \rightarrow R5$	
Segment 3 (Add)	$(R4 + R5) \rightarrow R6$		

The table in Figure 4.4 shows the contents of registers after each clock pulse. The three tasks, which are carried out nine times (27 suboperations), are completed in a total of 11 clock pulses.

In this example, the 27 tasks have been carried out in the period of 11 clock cycles giving a speed improvement of $27/11 = 2.45$ times, all other things being equal. The theoretical maximum speed improvement of a pipeline is equal to the number of segments, in this case three times.

4.2.2 Cache memory

MPU logic is usually faster than main memory access time, with the result that processing speed is limited primarily by the speed of main

Clock pulse number	Segment 1			Segment 2		Segment 3
	R1	**R2**	**R3**	**R4**	**R5**	**R6**
1	A1	B1	C1			
2	A2	B2	C2	A1 * B1	C1	
3	A3	B3	C3	A2 * B2	C2	A1 * B1 + C1
4	A4	B4	C4	A3 * B3	C3	A2 * B2 + C2
5	A5	B5	C5	A4 * B4	C4	A3 * B3 + C3
6	A6	B6	C6	A5 * B5	C5	A4 * B4 + C4
7	A7	B7	C7	A6 * B6	C6	A5 * B5 + C5
8	A8	B8	C8	A7 * B7	C7	A6 * B6 + C6
9	A9	B9	C9	A8 * B8	C8	A7 * B7 + C7
10				A9 * B9	C9	A8 * B8 + C8
11						A9 * B9 + C9

Figure 4.4   Table of register contents

memory. To overcome this, a special very-high-speed memory called a *cache* may be used. Cache memory increases the speed of processing, by making current programs and data available to the MPU at a rapid rate. The access time of cache memory may be up to seven times faster than main memory. It may either be part of the MPU (on board) or separate but intimately connected to the MPU.

The cache is used for storing segments of programs currently being executed and temporary data frequently needed in ongoing calculations. An important design consideration is that it must be possible to search the cache very efficiently, since the search takes place on every memory reference.

As an example; the Motorola 68030 has a 256-byte onboard instruction cache and a 256-byte onboard data cache. Both are direct-mapped caches, which means that each word of memory has a unique location within the cache. Direct-mapped caches, although smaller, are organised very much like main memory.

4.2.3   Overlapped register windows

There is often a need for subroutines called from the main program to pass values, either to the main program or other associated subroutines. This can be done by allocating a block of main memory for this purpose. However, in order to avoid the necessity for main memory access, processors may be designed with a relatively large number of registers. Some of these are used for passing variables from one routine to another. This arrangement is known as overlapped register windows.

Figure 4.5 shows the organization of a *register file* of 74 registers, which are divided into three groups. There are 10 global registers, four

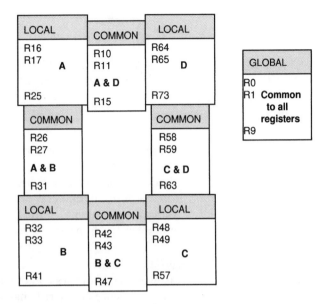

Figure 4.5 Overlapped register windows

groups of 10 local registers, and four groups of six registers which are common to two local groups.

This arrangement of registers conveniently corresponds to the requirements of high level languages such as C and Pascal. That is:

(i) Global registers provide for global variables.
(ii) Local registers provide for local variables.
(iii) Common registers are used for exchanging parameters and results without the necessity for accessing main memory.

The total number of registers available to each window, known as the window size, is given by:

$$\text{GLOBAL} + \text{LOCAL} + 2 \times \text{COMMON} = 10 + 10 + 2 \times 6 = 32$$

(Figure 4.5).

4.2.4 MPU timing and control

Pulses from a master clock generator are applied to all bistables and registers including those in the control unit. The contents of registers, however, only change state if they are enabled by signals from the control unit. There are two major types of control organisation, hardwired and microprogrammed.

Microprogrammed control
With microprogrammed control the microprogram is stored in an integral ROM. The basic system is shown in Figure 4.6 where an

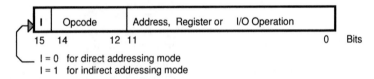

Figure 4.6   Microprogrammed control organization

external instruction causes a sequence of microinstructions to be read from the ROM.

Each microinstruction is transferred to the control data register, which provides both internal and external control signals.

Microprogrammed control is generally used in processors where complex instructions are to be implemented.

Hardwired control
Hardwired control uses combinational logic, together with timing pulses from a sequence counter. It has the advantage of generally being faster, but it is more suited to simple, fixed length instructions like Figure 4.7.

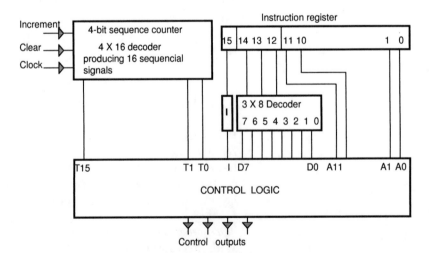

Figure 4.7   Typical fixed length instruction

The hardwired system shown in Figure 4.8 will decode and produce control signals from the fixed length microprocessor instructions. These instructions have a three-field format of mode, opcode and address.

Figure 4.8   Example of hardware control

4.3 Complex instruction set computer (CISC)

The design of an instruction set for a computer must take into consideration both machine language constructs and the requirements of high level programming languages. One way to improve the overall computer performance is to provide complex machine code instructions so that the compilation of code from a high level language is made simpler.

The major characteristics of CISC processors are:

(i) A large number of instructions, typically up to 250.
(ii) Instructions which perform specialised tasks and are used infrequently.
(iii) Typically 5 to 20 different addressing modes.
(iv) Variable length instruction formats.
(v) Instructions that manipulate operands in memory.
(vi) Specialized instructions which provide for some high level language procedures, and hence reduce the machine code requirement.
(vii) Microcode instruction execution.

As an example of a CISC MPU the main features of the MC68000 are listed in the next section.

4.3.1 The Motorola 68000 MPU (copyright of Motorola, used by permission)

The MC68000 CISC MPU has the following notable features:

(i) 32-bit internal data paths and registers.
(ii) 16-bit external data bus. The upper (D8 to D15) and lower (D0 to D7) bytes of the data bus have separate strobe signal lines, UDS and LDS respectively, to give easier control of 8-bit devices.
(iii) A1 to A23, 24-bit address bus providing the possibility of addressing 2^{24} (16 Mbyte), or 4 Mbyte words. The logic state of A0, which is only required for byte operation, is signalled by asserting LDS or UDS. LDS = 1 if A0 = 1 and UDS = 1 if A0 = 0.
(iv) The separation of registers into eight data registers and seven memory address registers.
(v) *Synchronous* or *asynchronous*[1] bus transfer. Synchronous bus transfer is used in systems containing, for example, 6800 devices which do not have an asynchronous mode.
(vi) Microcode instruction execution.
(vii) There are two modes of operation called *user* and *supervisor*, selected by function codes on control lines FC0, FC1 and FC2.

---

[1] Synchronous data transfer is when the clock controls data transfer operations and all transfers take a specific number of clock periods. Asynchronous data transfer is the transfer period terminated on the receipt of an acknowledge signal (in the case of the 68000 this is called DTACK). This allows a system to include devices with a wide range of access times.

Supervisor mode is a privileged level of operation, for use for instance with operating systems. Some especial instructions and registers are available in this mode.

(viii) Memory mapped I/O.

(ix) Many instructions can operate on bytes, words, or long words[2], indicated by attaching .B, .W or .L respectively to the operation mnemonic.

(x) Assembly language instructions have the opposite general format to that of the Z80:

operation ⟨source operand⟩, ⟨destination operand⟩

(xi) Fourteen addressing modes: register direct, register indirect, absolute, program counter relative, immediate and implied.

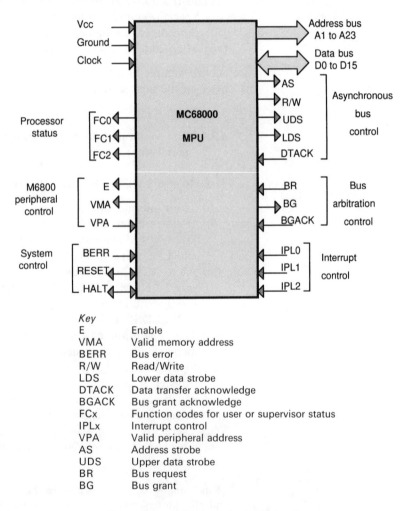

Figure 4.9 68000 input/output signals

---

[2] Byte = 8 bits, word = 16 bits, long word = 32 bits.

4.4 Reduced instruction set computer (RISC)

The concept of RISC architecture attempts to reduce execution time, with the aim of achieving one operation per clock cycle, by simplifying the instruction set. The major characteristics of a RISC MPU are:

(i) A simple instruction format with relatively few instructions.
(ii) Relatively few addressing modes, i.e. register, immediate and relative.
(iii) Relatively large numbers of registers to facilitate the processing of operations within the registers of the MPU.
(iv) Overlapped register windows.
(v) Memory references limited to load and store instructions.
(vi) Single clock cycle instruction execution with the use of pipelining.
(vii) Hardwired rather than microprogrammed control.

As an example of a RISC MPU the main features of the 32-bit MC88100 are listed in the following section.

4.4.1 The Motorola MC88100 (copyright of Motorola, used by permission)

The notable features of the Motorola MC88100 RISC MPU are listed below:

(i) 32-bit registers, data and address bus.
(ii) 32 general-purpose registers.
(iii) Separate data and instruction memory ports.
(iv) Pipeline load and store operations.
(v) Fifty-one instructions, effective one-cycle execution by the use of instruction pipelining.
(vi) Fixed length 4-byte instructions.
(vii) Hardwired instruction implementation.
(viii) Supervisor and user modes of operation.

The hardware connections to facilitate the features listed above are shown in Figure 4.10.

4.5 Single chip microcontrollers

The processors described so far are designed to form part of multi-chip systems, which require external memory for their operation. In addition to the registers, ALU, etc. of the MPU, the *single chip* microcontroller also contains RAM and ROM and possibly an Analogue to Digital Converter (ADC[3]) and a timer.

The example processor in this section is the Philips 83/87C752 (8XC752).

---

[3] For an explanation of ADC see Chapter 11.

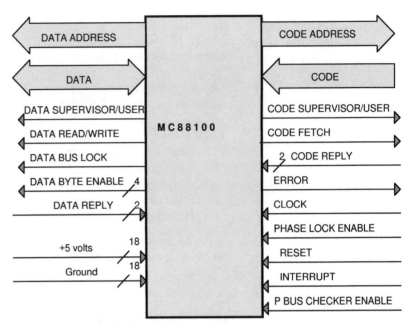

Figure 4.10   MC88100 input/output signals

4.5.1   The Philips 83/87C752 (8XC752) microcontroller (information used by kind permission of Philips Semiconductors and Signetics)

The 8XC752 is a CMOS[4], single chip, 8-bit microcontroller. The main features of this IC are listed below and the input/output signals are shown in Figure 4.11. This device has a 28-pin package with many of the pins having two or three functions.

The 8XC752 is used as an applications example in Chapter 5. Where additional information is included.

The main features of the 8XC752 are:

(i) Twenty-one input/output lines using three ports (0, 1 and 3).
(ii) Onboard clock oscillator with possible frequencies from 3.5 MHz to 16 MHz. The oscillator frequency may be derived from an external crystal.
(iii) Onboard memory consisting of:
Programming memory 2K × 8-bit ROM (83C752) or EPROM[5] (87C752)
Data memory 64 × 8 bits RAM
Special function register 128 bytes.
(iv) Five channel 8-bit analogue to digital converters. A to D conversion takes 40 machine cycles (40 μs with a 2 MHz clock).
(v) 16-bit auto-reloadable counter timer.

[4] CMOS   complementary metal oxide semiconductor.
[5] The EPROM version is usually used for application development.

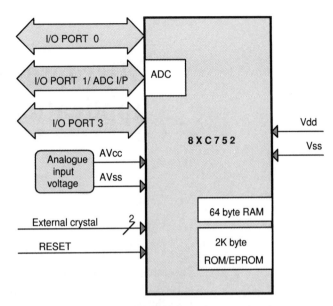

Figure 4.11 8XC752 input/output signals

    (vi) I^2C[6] serial bus I/O. Allows operation as a master or slave device on a I^2C small area network.

  (vii) 8-bit pulse width modulation (PWM) output.

 (viii) Seven fixed priority interrupts.

The connections shown in Figure 4.11 are the normal run-time signals. Memory programming is carried out via the I/O ports.

[6] I^2C Philips inter-integrated circuit bus system.

5 Microprocessor applications

5.1 Control and instrumentation systems – the airflow meter.

5.2 Communication systems – digital signal processing.

5.3 Commercial systems – desktop computer.

This chapter describes three microprocessor applications from three different electronic engineering spheres.

In Section 5.1 a microcontroller is used to measure and, to a limited extent, control airflow. This has been selected as it is an easy system to understand and would make an interesting project. The hardware is minimal and could be constructed on strip-board. Although programming could be carried out using the microcontroller's assembly language, the chip manufacturers recommend software development using C. Unfortunately a special C compiler must be acquired for this.

For the communications application of Section 5.2, a method of digital signal processing is described. This again offers the possibilities of an interesting project for those wishing to obtain further experience in the radio frequency/digital field.

Most of the practical exercises, in later chapters, assume the use of a personal computer (PC), so in Section 5.3 the basic features of this general-purpose machine are described.

5.1 Control and instrumentation systems – the airflow meter

(extracts from Applications Note AN429 by kind permission of Philips Semiconductors and Signetics)

The information in this section is taken from Philips Semiconductors Microcontroller Products Applications Note AN429. This applications note describes a low cost airflow measurement device based on the Philips 83/87C752[1] microcontroller. The design of the airflow meter includes sensors which allow the 8XC752 to measure three parameters: air velocity, pressure and temperature. The software compensates the measured air flow for both temperature and relative pressure. The control panel of the meter should look like Figure 5.1.

[1] The 83/87C752 was introduced in Chapter 4.

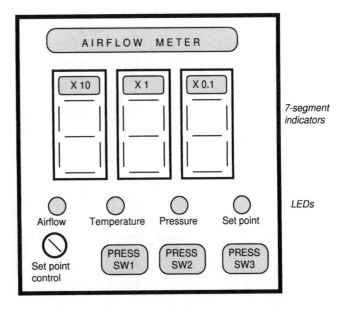

Figure 5.1   Airflow control panel

LED	Measurement	Switch
Airflow	Airflow in cubic feet per minute (CFM)	None
Temperature (°C)	Air temperature in degrees C	SW1
Pressure	Air pressure in pounds per square inch (PSI)	SW2
Set point	Setting of high or low airflow alarm	SW3

Figure 5.2   Panel operations

5.1.1   Hardware construction

Figure 5.2 is a table showing the control panel operation. Set point (SP) is a particular airflow which may be selected to give an alarm, or take some other action. The system software may be written to use set point for: air flow too high, air flow too low, or air flow equal to a given value.

The set point adjustment is a screwdriver control on the front panel. The airflow meter display circuit diagram is shown in Figure 5.3.

Figure 5.3 is an example of a **multiplexed display** circuit in which there are four elements, comprising three 7-segment indicators and four discrete LEDs (CFM, Temp, PSI and SP). The discrete LEDs are connected so that they form one element of the display.

These four elements all share a common, 8-bit data bus derived from port 3 of the processor, via high current drivers and current limiting resistors. The four elements are multiplexed using signals from Port 0 of

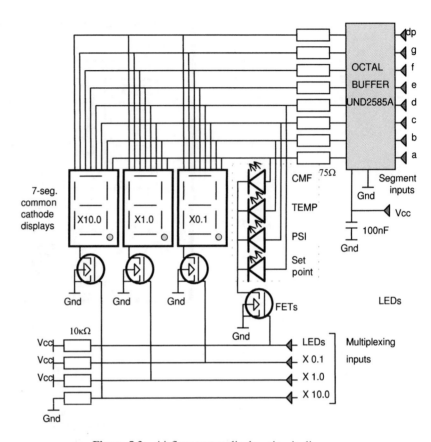

Figure 5.3   Airflow meter display circuit diagram

the processor, which effectively connects the common cathode of each display element in turn to ground via a FET[2] when data for that element is present at Port 3.

A diagram of the complete system is shown in Figure 5.4. The signals sent to processor terminals 1.3 and 1.4 when pushbuttons are pressed are shown in the table of Figure 5.5. The table in Figure 5.6 shows the configuration of Port 1 and the applied input signals.

5.1.2   Software development

The airflow meter software is almost entirely written in the high level language C, using a development package[3]. The program consists of a main program, main(), and four interrupt-driven routines. A flowchart of function main() is shown in Figure 5.7.

---

[2] FET   field effect transistor.
[3] Software should be available from several companies.

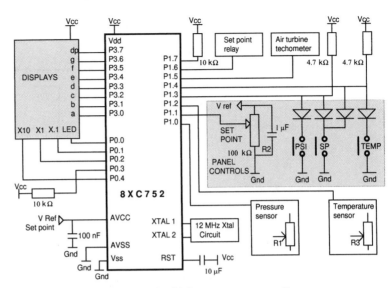

Figure 5.4   Airflow meter system diagram

		Button	**Quantity**
Port 1.3	**Port 1.4**	**pressed**	**measured**
HIGH	HIGH	NONE	Airflow
LOW	HIGH	SW1	Temperature
HIGH	LOW	SW2	Air pressure
LOW	LOW	SW3	Setpoint

Figure 5.5   Switching table

	Signal	**Inputs**	**Port 1**
Pin	**Configuration**	**Quantity**	**Comment**
1.0	ADC input 0	Air pressure sensor	The system measures air pressure relative to atmospheric pressure. The pressure sensor KP100A outputs a voltage difference, which is amplified to give a value (between Vss and Vdd). It is calibrated using R1
1.1	ADC input 1	Setpoint	Setpoint is a voltage adjusted by R2
1.2	ADC input 2	Air temperature	The temperature sensor produces an absolute voltage proportional to temperature. The sensor circuit includes an amplifier which sets the voltage between AVss and AVdd. The sensor output is calibrated using R3
1.3	Logic input	Pushbutton	The three switches select one of four logic conditions, as shown in the
1.4		switches	table of Figure 5.5
1.5	Logic input	Airflow	Measurement of air velocity is by an air turbine tachometer connected via an optoisolator
1.6	Logic output	Relay control	The relay may be used to operate an alarm or take some other action to protect equipment

Figure 5.6   Port 1 signal inputs

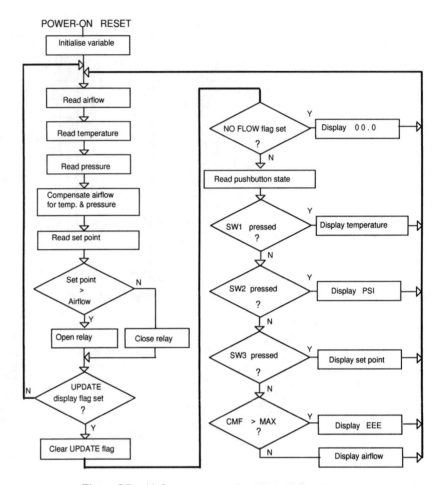

Figure 5.7   Airflow meter, main program flow diagram

The display is determined by the pushbutton state and the NOFLOW flag. If the flow exceeds a value of 30CMF, EEE is displayed as an error indicator.

The four interrupt routines are:

INT 3 Multiplex()   Refreshes the display.
INT 6 ReadSwitch()   Indicates if a switch has been pressed.
INT 0 CalcCFM()   Calculates the airflow.
INT 1 Overflow()   Indicates an overflow.

INT 3 Multiplex( )

Free running; Timer 1 generates an interrupt on INT 3 approximately every millisecond. This is used in a round robin multiplex of the four LED display elements by asserting P0.0, P0.1, P02 and P0.4 in turn, thus refreshing each display element about every 4 ms.

INT 6 ReadSwitch( )

The pulse width modulation (PWM) prescaler is configured to generate a 10.3 ms periodic interrupt on INT 6. After 32 interrupts an UPDATE flag is SET, causing the switch input to be read and the display updated every 330 ms.

INT 0 CalcCFM( )

Air velocity is determined by the elapse time between interrupts on INT 0, which is associated with Timer 0. Timer 0 clocks the lower 16 bits of a 24 bit register at 1MHz. Thus the register stores the time in microseconds (μs).

INT 1 Overflow( )

If the elapse time on INT 0 is too long, causing the upper 8 bits of Timer 0 register to become too large, the NOFLOW flag is set. When this is detected 00.0 will be displayed.

5.2 Communication systems – digital signal processing (DSP)

This section describes how a microprocessor is used for signal processing[4]. Specialised hardware ICs may be used for DSP, which in general will have a higher operating speed; however, for greater flexibility specialised DSP microprocessors are a useful alternative. *Real time* calculations have to be carried out on signals, therefore onboard multiplication and division functions are an essential requirement of DSP microprocessors. In order to maintain high speed operations, the modern DSP IC will also have onboard memory in the form of RAM, ROM and cache. It may also contain both parallel and serial ports. These specialised ICs are available from *Texas Instruments*, who also produce DSP Starter Kits for development purposes. To illustrate how DSP may be used, Figure 5.10 shows a block diagram of an *amplitude modulated* (AM)[5] *single sideband* (SSB)[6] receiver, and Figure 5.11 is a version where DSP is used for filtering the signals.

Referring to Figure 5.10, after preselection by the *bandpass filter* (BPF), the incoming signal is split and fed to the I and Q[7] mixers. The

---

[4] Signal processing is the technique of selecting, filtering and amplifying communications signals.

[5] Amplitude modulation is where information to be transmitted is used to vary the amplitude of a carrier wave. The carrier wave is a constant amplitude sine wave. The frequency of the carrier must be constant and much higher than the highest modulating frequency.

[6] With basic *amplitude modulation* two *sidebands* and a *carrier* are produced, Figure 5.8. This system is good for simple receiver design and operation, but it is very wasteful as far as power and channel spacing are concerned. As both sidebands carry the same information it is only really necessary to transmit one of them. Single sideband (SSB) modulation, Figure 5.9, only produces either a lower sideband (LSB) or an upper sideband (USB).

[7] I and Q are generally used to indicate in-phase and quadrature channels. The phase of Q is either +90° or −90° with respect to I.

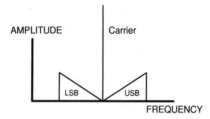

Figure 5.8   AM – amplitude/frequency diagram

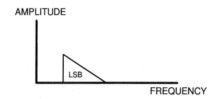

Figure 5.9   SSB – amplitude/frequency diagram

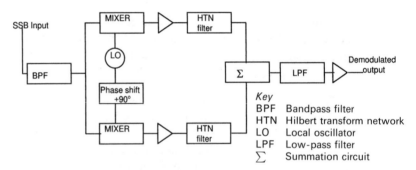

Figure 5.10   SSB phasing type demodulator

sinusoidal signal from a local oscillator (LO) is fed directly to the I mixer, and via a 90° phase shifter to the Q mixer. The audio frequency outputs of the mixers are fed to the Hilbert transform networks (HTN) after amplification. When the two signals from the HTNs are applied to the summation circuit ($\sum$), the phase shifts introduced by the mixers and filters cause the cancellation of one and the addition of the other sideband. The demodulated signal is finally passed through a low-pass filter (LPF) and amplified.

Figure 5.11 is a modification of Figure 5.10 showing the substitution of a digital signal processor in place of the filtering and summation circuits.

Figure 5.12 shows a system diagram of the main elements of a DSP receiver.

In Figure 5.12, after signal selection, the I and Q signals are applied to ADCs[8].

---

[8] An analogue signal may be a simple sine wave or a complex waveform having many sinusoidal components. Analogue signals may have any value between a minimum and a maximum limit. Types of ADC are covered in Chapter 11.

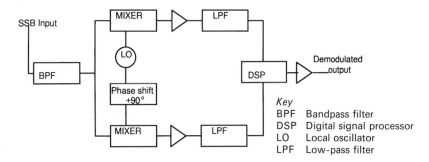

Figure 5.11 SSB with a DSP filter

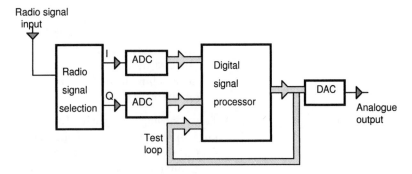

Figure 5.12 DSP system diagram

The ADCs, which include sample and hold[9] circuits, sample the analogue signal at a frequency which is at least twice the highest input frequency[10]. The conversion clock frequency will depend on both the type of ADC and the number of output bits. The analogue output is obtained from the digital to analogue converter (DAC[11]).

The digital filtering system process digitally encodes samples taken at discrete time intervals. These samples represent instantaneous values of the analogue input waveform. The basis of most digital filtering is a process of averaging successive samples, which are then weighted[12] as necessary to produce the required filter characteristic. Although this DSP version of a single sideband demodulator is more complex than its analogue equivalent, it has two main advantages:

(i) By changing the software, it offers the possibility of being used to demodulate other modes of modulation.

---

[9] When converting a time-varying analogue signal it is necessary to hold the sample for the period of conversion.

[10] This is necessary to prevent **aliasing**, which is a form of distortion introduced by sampling.

[11] See Chapter 10 for an explanation of DACs.

[12] Weighting is a process of multiplying a value by a given factor.

(ii) It is possible to achieve certain filter specifications which are either difficult or impossible using normal analogue circuit.

5.3   Commercial systems – the desktop computer

Desktop computers, with a useful performance for both home and commercial purposes, have been available since the early 1980s.

The personal computer (PC) refers to the IBM designed desktop computer. This machine has been constantly developed and improved over the past 20 years, in line with the development of the Intel microprocessor. Three reasons for the popularity of the PC are:

(i)   Advertising – both the PC itself and the associated Microsoft operating system.
(ii) A very wide range of application software.
(iii) The hardware architecture which increases the versatility of this general-purpose machine by allowing the user to select from a wide range of modules in the form of plug-in circuit boards. This allows the machine to be fairly inexpensively customised according to user requirements.

When choosing computers for an electronics applications laboratory, point (iii) above was one of the main reasons for the author's preference for PCs. Cards[13], directly plugged into the PC motherboard, included programmable parallel I/O interface[14], IEEE comms, transputer and networking.

5.3.1   The system

The digital components of desktop computers, like the PC, have similar layouts. The hardware is designed around a particular microprocessor using a bus system. Figure 5.14 shows common components of the system, and the back of a typical PC is illustrated in Figure 5.13.

In the case of the PC, most of the essential components, including the MPU, ROM and RAM, are accommodated on a motherboard. Edge connector sockets[15] are also installed on the motherboard, which provide connections to the control, data and address buses. Various application cards may be plugged into these edge connectors.

When the computer is first switched on, it will initially read *start-up* instructions from the ROM. It then loads into RAM the operating system, which is usually stored on the hard disk. The final step in the start-up process is to load an applications program from the hard disk, floppy disk or CD.

Generally at least one parallel printer port and one serial port are provided. The parallel printer port may also be used for high speed data

---

[13] Cards are printed circuit boards complete with chips and external connectors.
[14] See Chapter 9 for parallel interfacing.
[15] Edge connectors used in this way are often referred to as **slots**.

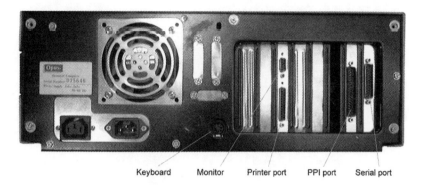

Keyboard   Monitor   Printer port   PPI port   Serial port

Figure 5.13   Personal computer ports

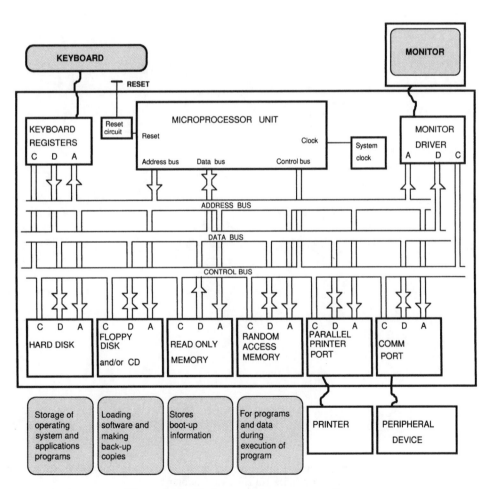

Figure 5.14   Desktop computer system diagram

transfer from another machine. The serial port, often referred to as the *Comm* port is used for communication with peripherals[16] such as modems and plotters. A printer which accepts data either in *serial*[17] or parallel[18] form may be used.

[16] Peripherals – any ancillary devices electrically connected to the computer.
[17] For serial data transfer see Chapter 8.
[18] For parallel data transfer see Chapter 9.

6 Software design

6.1 Software development

6.2 Top down design

6.3 Structured programming

6.4 Pseudocode

6.5 Flowcharts

This chapter looks at the main principles of software design. The aim is to encourage the reader to do a little structured development before typing in the program code.

The most visible result of a software project is a working program, so there is often pressure to start coding immediately, especially with relatively short programs. Unfortunately, this usually leads to poorly structured programs that are likely to be difficult to maintain. If you have succumbed, as I think most of us do, to code a program directly, it is worthwhile doing a retrospective design. In this way you can check that the program conforms to general design principles.

With a systematic method of software development, more time is spent in earlier stages of program design. Code takes longer to appear, so the benefits are not always immediately appreciated. It should be remembered that the various methods of software design are developed from principles which have been found to work best, either for individuals or organisations. Software design itself is not an exact science, the idea is to use a method which produces a good, clearly written program.

6.1 Software development

In addition to the above points, structured programming including good documentation has the following advantages:

(i) If assistance is required to debug a program it is much more convenient if a structured design is available.

(ii) Large projects require team development, necessitating that programming be decomposed into independent parts.

(iii) Software is often maintained by people, other than the developers, who will need to appreciate the program structure.

One way to manage software development is to divide it into several subtasks, or phases. Following the establishment of the user or customer requirements, the five development phases, as shown in Figure 6.1,

Phase	Comment	Result
Analysis	The intention is to provide a clear understanding of what the system is about, and its underlying concepts	Specification document
Design	Defines how the specified behaviour is achieved	Structure chart or pseudo language program
Implementation	Encode the design in a programming language	Program code
Test sub-systems Debug functions	Test and debug the functions	Working functions
Test system Debugging Document	Test the complete system; hardware and software if appropriate	Working system

Figure 6.1   Subtasks of software development

should produce a working system. Each phase addresses different problems. The output from each phase is the basis for the next.

6.2   Top down design

In any top down process the idea is to start with the overall idea or device and then dissect it into smaller and smaller pieces. Top down program design provides a systematic method of analysing a programming task. A structure chart is produced in the form of a tree diagram, each row showing the component parts of the box immediately above, see Figure 6.2.

Example (a)   Structure chart for temperature converter.

Draw a structure chart for a program to convert temperatures between the Celsius, Fahrenheit and Kelvin scales.

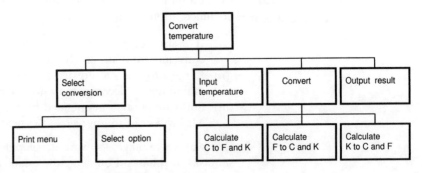

Figure 6.2   Structure chart for Example (a)

6.3 Structured programming

Rules for structured programming:

(i) Program modules should be small and clear enough to be comprehensible.

(ii) Program modules should have only one entry point at the beginning of the module, and one exit point at the end of the module.

(iii) Programs should use combinations of components chosen exclusively from three simple types of program constructs, namely:

sequences   two or more operations, one after the other

selections   choosing one component from two or more

iterations   repeat one or more operation until some condition is satisfied.

6.3.1 Jackson Structured Programming (JSP)

The JSP design technique uses four basic components:

(i) **Elementary** – no further subdivision into constituent components.

(ii) **Sequence** – two or more components occurring in order.

(iii) **Selection** – one component selected from a number of alternatives.

(iv) **Iteration** – a single component is repeated zero or more times.

Each component of a sequence, selection or iteration may be a sequence, selection or an iteration, so there is no limit to the complexity of the structure which can be formed.

Elementary
Elementary operations include the following:

Initialisation	Open files
	Program, programmable I/O ports
Program termination	Close files
	Exit to system
Input/Output	Input data from files or keyboard
	Output to screen or printer
Processing	Arithmetic and logic operations

Sequence
Figure 6.3 shows a sequence, ABC, divided into three components.

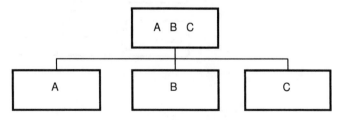

Figure 6.3 Sequence

Selection

The selection component indicates what choices are available when one single component is to be selected from several alternatives. A small circle in the boxes on the second row shows that ABC is a selection component and that only one of the three items shown is to be selected, Figure 6.4.

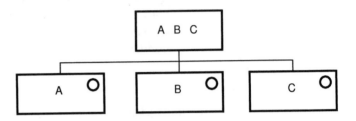

Figure 6.4   Selection

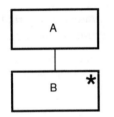

Figure 6.5   Iteration

Iteration

An iteration consists of one component which is repeated zero or more times. The diagram, Figure 6.5, shows process A, with iterated component B. The *asterisk* indicates that B is the component to be repeated zero or more times.

Example (b)   JSP chart

In Figure 6.6 the structure chart of Example (a) has been modified to incorporate the JSP rules. This JSP chart is summarised in the table of Figure 6.7.

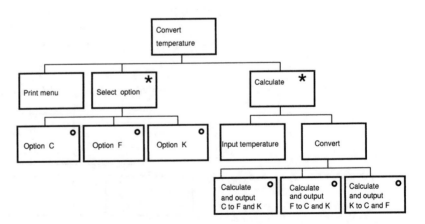

Figure 6.6   JSP chart

Component name	Component	Decomposition
Convert temperature	A sequence of three components	Print menu Select option Calculate
Print menu	Elementary component. Output to screen	None
Select option	A selection from three components	Option C Option F Option K
Calculate	An iteration and a sequence of two components	Input temperature Convert
Input temperature	Elementary component. Input from keyboard	None
Convert	A selection from three components	C to F and K F to C and K K to C and F
Calculate and output	Elementary component. Output calculation to screen	None

Figure 6.7 Summary of the JSP chart

6.4 Pseudo code (structured English)

Pseudo code, sometimes called structured English, is a useful tool in the process of developing a program, it may be used in the following circumstances:

(i)   As an intermediate step between a diagrammatic program design specification and the implementation language.
(ii) Directly to describe processing algorithms.
(iii) In the documentation of a program to describe its logic using a formal notation.

Converting a program design written in *pseudo* code into a *high level language* such as C is a relatively straightforward matter. The conventions used in C are used in the following components.

Both selection and iteration may depend on an *expression* for their implementation. Relational, bitwise and logical operators which may be used in expressions are listed below. Each operator compares value x to value y, i.e. $x > y$.

Relational operators

<	less than
<=	less than or equal to
=>	greater than or equal to
>	greater than

!=	not equal to
==	equal to

Bitwise operators

&	bitwise AND
|	bitwise OR
^	bitwise XOR
<<	left shift
>>	right shift
~	1's complement (unitary operator)[1]

Logical operators

These operators which evaluate to either 0 (false) or 1 (true) are:

&&	AND
||	OR

6.4.1   Sequence

Sequence components may be either elementary lines of codes or complete functions. Functions will be defined by name at the beginning of the program.

6.4.2   Selection

A specified component is selected from two or more components. Two forms of selection may be used:

(i)   Using **if else**. Note: the *else* part is optional

```
if (expression)
      statement1
else
      statement2
```

(ii) Using switch and case

```
switch (expression)
{
      case value1 : statement1
      case value2 : statement2
      case value3 : statement3
      case valuen : statementn
}
```

---

[1] ~ changes 1s to 0s and 0s to 1s.

6.4.3   Iteration

There are two alternatives:

(i)   Using **while** for an indefinite number of iterations

> **while** (expression)
>   statement

For an iteration which continues for ever use

> **while (1)**

(ii)   Using **for** for a defined number of iterations

> **for**(start value;end + 1 value; increment value)
>   statement

If **i** is a defined variable, and the *iteration* is to be from 0 to 10, the **for** iteration has the form

> **for**(i = 0 ; i < 11 ; i++)

Example (c)   Pseudo code.

This example is a pseudo code version of the JSP chart of Figure 6.6:

```
main component
    print select option C, F or K
    input selection
    switch(selection)
    {
        case C   :CalcCon(1)
        case F   :CalcCon(2)
        case K   :CalcCon(3)
    }
CalcCon(variable)            /*Calculate conversion variable = 1, 2 or 3*/
    {
        input temperature
        switch(variable)
        {
                case 1      : print {calculation of F and K}
                case 2      : print {calculation of C and K}
                case 3      : print {calculation of C and F}
        }
    }while(temperature != exit value)
```

6.5   Flowcharts   Flowcharts are a useful aid when describing how a program works. The chart is specifically used to convey, in diagrammatic form, the logic, processing operation, and flow of control of the program. The flowchart is completely independent of programming languages, it works just as well with machine code or a high level language.

Example (d)   Flowchart.

Figure 6.8 shows a flowchart for the temperature conversion example. The full C program for this example can be found in Chapter 7.

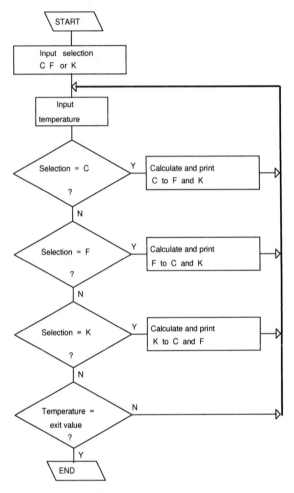

Figure 6.8   Flowchart for Example (a)

7 Programming in C

The interfacing ideas and exercises in this book are designed to appeal to engineering students, hence the selection of a popular, professional engineering computer language to implement the software part of exercises. C was first created by Bell Laboratories in the 1970s. During the 1980s C has been developed and has become the preferred modern-day language. There are a number of books which deal with C in depth, and the reader would be well advised to study one of these in due course. This chapter is designed to provide sufficient information for the reader to undertake exercises described in subsequent chapters.

Before proceeding further it is worth noting two important points about program files:

(i) Always save the source and executable file of each program you write.
(ii) As you will eventually have a large number of programs, it is important to use program names which help to identify each program (names like fred or progname should be avoided). Program names have a maximum of eight characters.

7.1 An introduction to C

High level languages such as C compile an executable file of binary machine code instructions which are only understood by the microprocessor for which they are written. To write a program in C you must have the correct C software installed on the computer. This will usually be a package which includes a *text editor*, *library files*, *compiler*, *linker*, *help files* and *example programs*.

Portability means that a program written on one system will run on another system which uses the same microprocessor. C programs are generally more portable than programs written in other languages. If modifications are necessary, and if the program is well written, they can usually be made just by changing a few lines of code at the beginning of the program. C compilers are available for many systems, from 8-bit microprocessors to supercomputers.

C is a programmer oriented language, it gives access to hardware, and it allows for the manipulation of individual bits in memory. It has a large selection of operators that allow succinct expressions. Tasks such as converting forms of data tend to be simpler in C than some other languages. C also has a large library of useful functions which fulfil needs commonly facing programmers.

Lastly, make use of the *help* file. It is a good idea to look at the help file every time you use an unfamiliar function. The help file will show the header files required for each function.

7.2   Eight steps to programming in C

Step 1   Define the program objectives (user requirements)

Write down in general terms:

(i)   What you want the program to do?
(ii)   What input (information) does your program require?
(iii)   Specify any calculations and manipulation of numbers or text.
(iv)   Specify the output you require from the program.

Step 2   Design the program

Use one of the design methods described in Chapter 6.

Step 3   Write the code

This is the process of translating the program ideas into C language. A text editor is used to create what is called a *source code* file. This file contains the C rendition of your program. Listing 7.3.1 shows an example of C source code. Comments are enclosed with /*comment*/. Nested comments are not allowed. All functions, written as part of the program, apart from main(), are listed at the beginning of the program. All variables must be declared either before main(), if they are to be available to all functions, in which case they are called **global**, or at the beginning of each function, in this case they are known as **local**. The data type (int, char, float, etc.) of the variable must be specified.

At this stage the program is given a name with an extension, **.c**. The program in Listing 7.3.1 could be named **ascii.c**.

Step 4   Compile

The compiler's job is to convert source code into machine binary code. Different microprocessors have different machine code languages. So the compiler must convert the source file into the machine language of the object microprocessor.

The compiler produces a file which will be saved with as ⟨*name*⟩.**obj**. So when Listing 7.3.1 is compiled it will be called **ascii.obj**.

Step 5 Linking

If the program was compiled without errors, the linker is run to produce an executable file.

The linker has three jobs:

 (i) To combine the necessary start-up code for the system being used.
 (ii) To combine library files into the final program.
(iii) To combine any other files which have been previously written.

If all the necessary files are present the linker will produce a file with extension **.exe** (for Listing 7.3.1 this is **ascii.exe**).

Step 6 Run the program

This is generally achieved by just typing the program name without the extension, hence **ascii** for Listing 7.3.1. With some programs, such as those which input data from a file, it may be necessary to provide test data before the program is run.

Step 7 Test and debug the program

It is important to check that the program does what it is supposed to do. Some of the checks are listed below:

  (i) Does it input the whole range of data correctly?
 (ii) How does it respond to incorrect data?
(iii) Is the output in accordance with the design?
 (iv) Does it leave the computer in a correct running state?
  (v) Will the program run repeatedly?
 (vi) Does it interfere with any other software including the computer operating system?

Step 8 Maintain and modify the program

When programs are brought into use they often require some modification to overcome unforeseen problems which include:

  (i) Errors caused by untested data entries.
 (ii) The inclusion of another feature.
(iii) Adaptation of the program to run on a different computer system.

In order that a program may be maintained, that is, be modified or have minor bugs removed, it is important that it is well documented when written.

7.3 Writing C programs

Referring to Listing 7.3.1

(i) The program begins with a comment enclosed by /* */ , which gives the program name, its aim and any other relevant details such as the date it was written and the program writer's name. Comments give the reader information about the program they are ignored by the compiler.

(ii) Header files required by functions included in the program follow next. Each header file is preceded by #**include**. Header files are linked to the program.

(iii) In this simple program the function main() is now written. All programs must contain **main()**, the *void* in front of main indicates that no variables are to be passed at the end of main().

(iv) On the next line there is the **opening *brace*** of main(). All functions must have an opening and closing brace. It is good practice, and makes programs easier to read, if statements enclosed by braces are indented.

(v) After the opening brace any *local variables* must be declared. Local variable are variables used in the function in which they are declared. Hence **int character** defines an *integer variable* called *character*.

(vi) **printf()** sends the text enclosed by quotes to the screen. Note \n moves the screen cursor to a new line.

(vii) **getch()** waits for an input from the keyboard and stores it under the label character.

(viii) **printf()** in the penultimate line sends the text in quotes to the screen, it also substitutes the 'character' input for **%c** and the ASCII code of the character for **%i**.

(ix) Finally, the **closing brace** of the main function.

```
/*ascii.c Program outputs the ASCII code of the character entered*/
#include  < stdio.h >  /*header file for printf()*/
void main()
{
    int character;
    printf("\nEnter a character. ");
    character = getch();
    printf("\nThe ASCII code of %c is %i ",character,character);
}
```

Listing 7.3.1   ascii.c

7.4 Debugging the program

Debugging is the process of finding and fixing program errors. There are three main stages where errors may show up:

(i)   When it is compiled to produce the .obj file.
(ii) When it is linked to produce the .exe file.
(iii) When it is run.

If the error messages are read carefully, the compiler will give considerable help with stage (i). The two main reasons why a program will not compile are either *typing errors* or *syntax errors*. A syntax error occurs when C rules are not complied with.

Figure 7.1 is a table of typical errors which could occur in Listing 7.3.1. Note some errors produce more than one error message.

7.4.1 Typical errors

Line	Error	Error message or result
void main();	Semicolon after main()	Need an identifier to declare
int character	No semicolon after character	Declaration syntax error
printf(\nEnter a character. ");	missing " before \n	Illegal character \ Unidentified symbol 'nEnter' Function call missing) Unterminated string
Character = getch();	Capital C at the beginning of character. The system is case sensitive	Undefined symbol
printf("The ASCII code of %c is i% \n", character,character);	i% instead of %i	This produces a run time error. i% will be printed instead of the ASCII code
printf("The ASCII code of %c is i% \n", character);	The second character label is missing	This produces a run time error and prints 0 instead of the ASCII code

Figure 7.1 Typical errors

7.5 Program examples and exercises

The following series of programs will introduce many more functions and procedures.

7.5.1 Exercise – output of strings, printf()

The **printf()** function may be used to print both strings and the values of variables. The listing and screen output are shown below.

NOTES:

(i) The label MILES is **defined** as 26.
(ii) The label YARDS is **defined** as 385.
(iii) A variable labelled km is declared as float, meaning floating point number. This reserves 4 bytes of memory.
(iv) % = format conversion.
(v) %f print floating point in decimal format.

```
/*string.c   Output of strings*/
#include <stdio.h>
#define MILES 26
#define YARDS 385
void main()
{
    float km;                              /*Declaration of variable, km*/
    km = 1.609 * (MILES + YARDS/1760.0);        /*Calculate km*/
    printf("\n A marathon is %f kilometres\n\n",km);
}
```

Listing 7.5.1   string.c

```
A marathon is 42.185970 kilometres
```

Figure 7.2   Screen output of Listing 7.5.1

Questions

A   What form does **%e** give the answer in?
B   The field length and the number of decimal places may be specified
    by placing a number between **%** and **f**. What output will **%4.2f**
    produce?

7.5.2   Exercise – print the bytes reserved for variables

This program uses the C function **sizeof()** to show the number of bytes
reserved for the variable types. Compile and run the program. Both the
listing and screen output are given below.

```
/*size.c   This program prints out the number of bytes allocated to the
various types*/
#include <stdio.h>
void main()
{
    printf("\n");
    printf("TYPE SIZE IN BYTES\n");
    printf("char      %d\n", sizeof(char));
    printf("int       %d\n", sizeof(int));
    printf("long      %d\n", sizeof(long));
    printf("float     %d\n", sizeof(float));
    printf("double    %d\n", sizeof(double));
}
```

Listing 7.5.2   size.c

TYPE	SIZE IN BYTES
char	1
int	2
long	4
float	4
double	8

Figure 7.3   Screen output of Listing 7.5.2

7.5.3   Exercise – number converter

Convert denary to hexadecimal, and hexadecimal to denary. The following points should be noted:

(i) The **scanf**() function provides input from the keyboard. The input to this function is terminated with a carriage return (CR). **%d** instructs scanf() to read a decimal number. The *ampersand* (&) in front of the variable label is a requirement for using this function with number input.

(ii) **%X** instructs scanf() to read a hexadecimal number, and printf() to print in hexadecimal format.

```
/*number.c   Using scanf() for the input of data*/
#include < stdio.h >
void main()
{
    int datain;
    printf("Enter a denary whole number ");
    scanf ("%d",&datain);
    printf("\n%d denary = %X hexadecimal\n\n",datain,datain);
    printf("\n\nEnter a hexadecimal number ");
    scanf ("%X",&datain);
    printf("\n%X hexadecimal = %d denary \n\n",datain,datain);
}
```

Listing 7.5.3   number.c

The output to the screen for the following inputs is shown in Figure 7.4:

denary number   **25**
hexadecimal number   **a4**.

```
Enter a denary whole number   25
25 denary = 19 hexadecimal
Enter a hexadecimal number   a4
A4 in hexadecimal = 164 denary
```

Figure 7.4   Screen output of Listing 7.5.3

7.5.4   Exercise – clear the screen

There is often a requirement to clear the screen during the running of a program. This may be achieved in several ways, depending on the system and the version of C being used. Here are three *clear screen* instructions, try them in turn in the previous program:

(i) After #include < stdio.h >   insert **#include < stdlib.h >**   when the screen is to be cleared insert **system("cls")**.
(ii) When the screen is to be cleared insert **printf("\033[2J")**.
(iii) After #include < stdio.h >   insert **#include   < conio.h >**   when the screen is to be cleared insert **clrscr()**.

7.5.5   Exercise – the for loop

This is an *iteration* exercise which makes use of the **for** loop. The screen output is shown in Figure 7.5 and the listing is given below. Note the following points:

(i) In the **for**() function:

    i is initialised, in this case to 1
    the maximum value of **i** is set, in this case to less than eleven
    the step value is set, in this case to i++, which means i = i + 1.
The items between braces will be executed until and including i = 10.
(ii) The 2 between % and d sets up a field of 2 digits.

```
/*for.c   Iteration using the 'for' loop*/
#include < stdio.h >
#include < stdlib.h >
void main()
{
   int i;
   float f = 1;                /*Initialises variable 'f' to 1*/
   system("cls");
   for(i = 1; i < 11; i++) /*Iteration*/
   {
       f = f * i;
       printf("\n%2d factorial = %.0f",i,f);
   }
}
```

Listing 7.5.5   for.c

```
 1 factorial = 1
 2 factorial = 2
 3 factorial = 6
 4 factorial = 24
 5 factorial = 120
 6 factorial = 720
 7 factorial = 5040
 8 factorial = 40320
 9 factorial = 362880
10 factorial = 3628800
```

Figure 7.5 Screen output of Listing 7.5.5

7.5.6 Exercise – square of numbers

A Write a program which prints the squares of numbers from 1 to 20.
B Write a program which inputs a number **n** and prints **n**^{2}. This program should repeat the process five times before it ends.

7.5.7 Exercise – store data in an array

Figure 7.6 is a structure chart for this exercise. The listing shows how to store data in an array. In this case the array is called **data** and the [21] indicates that 20 integers may be stored in the array, at positions data[0] to data[19]. Position [20] is reserved for the end of array character which is inserted automatically. Note the following points:

 (i) **%x** indicates input or print in hexadecimal number format.
 (ii) **\t** means tabulation.
 (iii) It is necessary to flush the input with the **fflush()** function otherwise the **scanf()** function will terminate the input if a non-hexadecimal character is pressed.

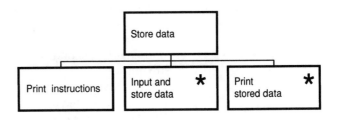

Figure 7.6 Structure chart for Listing 7.5.7

```
/*store.c   store data in an array */
#include <stdio.h>
#include <stdlib.h>
void main()
{
    int i;
    int data[21]; /*Declare an array which can store 20 integers in
        locations 0 to 19 */
    system("cls");
    printf("\nInput 20 hexadecimal numbers, Press Enter after each
        input\n\n");
    for(i=0; i<20; i++)
    {
        printf("%2d ",i+1);    /*print data at numbers from 1 to 20*/
        scanf("%X",&data[i]); /*store data array in position i*/
        fflush(stdin);           /*flush the input buffer*/
    }
    printf("\n\n\n Data input completed\n");
    for(i=0; i<20; i++)        /*read back the input*/
        printf("\n%d\t%x",i+1,data[i]);
}
```

Listing 7.5.7   store.c

7.5.8   Exercise – modifications to Exercise 7.5.7

A   Modify the program to enter and print data in denary.
B   Find the difference between using **%x** and **%X** in the **printf()** function.

7.5.9   Exercise – store data on disc

Figure 7.7 is a structure chart for this exercise. Note the following points:

(i)   This listing is divided into functions: main(), DataIn() and Disc-Store().
(ii)   Lower case is always used for C language functions supplied as part of the C package. The convention of using a mixture of upper and lower case for function names, written as part of the program, gives a convenient way of producing an easily readable program, with meaningful function names; it also ensures that prescribed words are not used.
(iii)   Change the number after TOTAL at the beginning of the program in order to change the number of bytes entered.
(iv)   The label *filename* is a local variable to **main()**, hence it has to be passed to the other functions.

(v) This program uses selection in the form of the **if()** function.

(vi) When a file is opened it is automatically given a number, called a *handle*. In this case it will be stored by the variable **fd**. The handle must always be used when referring to the file. There is an error if the file handle equals −1, hence the file handle is compared with −1, using (**fd** == −1). Note, if (fd = −1) was used, −1 would be assigned to fd.

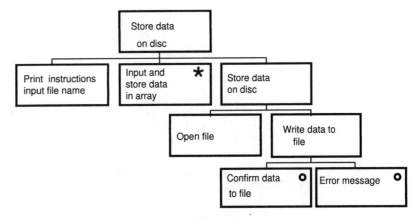

Figure 7.7   Structure chart for Listing 7.5.9

7.5.10   Exercise – testing Exercise 7.5.9

A   Check that the data has been correctly stored on the disc file.
   (i)   Run the program.
   (ii)   Input a recognisable series of hexadecimal numbers representing ASCII printable characters, such as:

   41 42 43 44 45 46 47 48 49 4a 4b 4c 4d 4e 4f 50 51 52 53.

   (iii)   Use the DOS[1] command **type** *filename* to display the contents of the file. If the input shown above is used you should see:

   ABCDEFGHIJKLMNOPQRST.

B   Use a read only disc to check the error statement 'Cannot create file'.

7.5.11   Exercise – load data from a disc file

Figure 7.8. is the structure chart for this listing. Note the following points:

[1] DOS   Disc Operating System.

```
/*discstor. c input data into an array, name and open a disc file
and copy the data to disc */
#include <stdio.h>
#include <dos.h>
#include <io.h>              /*to define the open function*/
#include <sys\stat.h>        /* to define S_IWRITE */
#define TOTAL 20             /* change the number of bytes by changing
                                            the number after TOTAL*/
char data[TOTAL+1];  /*define a global array*/
void DataIn(char[14]);   /*define functions*/
void DiscStore(char[14]);
void main()
{
    char filename[14];      /*stores the file name*/
    data[TOTAL+1]='/0';
    printf("\nInput and store data in an array\n");
    DataIn(filename);       /*calls DataIn and passes the file name*/
    DiscStore(filename);   /*calls DiscStore and passes the file name*/
}
void DataIn(char filename[14])
{
    int i;
    system("cls");
    printf("\n Input %i two digit hexadecimal numbers\n\n",TOTAL);
    for(i=0;i<TOTAL;i++)     /*Iteration*/
    {
        printf("%2d ",i+1);
        scanf(%X",&data[i]);
        fflush(stdin);
    }
    printf("\n\nEnter name of disc file ");
    scanf("%s",filename);
}
void DiscStore(char filename[14])
{
    int fd,bytes=0;
    fd = creat(filename,S_IWRITE); /* create or open a file */
    if(fd ==- 1)                             /*Selection*/
        printf("\n Cannot create file: %s",filename);
    else
        bytes = write(fd,data,TOTAL); /*write to file fd from array
                                            data TOTAL bytes*/
    if(bytes == =- 1)
        printf("No bytes written to file: %s",filename);
    else
        printf("\n %d written to file: %s",bytes,filename);
    close(fd);
}
```

Listing 7.5.9   discstor.c

(i)
The function DiscLoad() returns the actual number of *bytes* loaded. Only *one* variable can be returned from a function.

(ii) The program **discstor** must be executed first so that there is a file to read. Check that the error message is printed if there is no file to read.

(iii) In the **read()** line the number of bytes in the file is first determined using the **filelength()** function.

(iv) When the data is printed, any binary numbers with a 1 as the most significant bit will be assumed to be negative. In order to maintain the negative status, all vacant bits to the left will be filled with 1s and

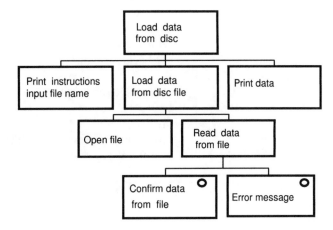

Figure 7.8   Structure chart for Listing 7.5.11

hence be printed with leading characters FF.

Listing 7.5.11   discload.c

```
/*discload.c load data from a disc file */
#include < stdio.h >          /*required for printf() and scanf() */
#include < stdlib.h >         /*required for system()*/
#include < io.h >             /*required for open() and read() */
#include < sys\stat.h >       /* to define S_IREAD */
int DiscLoad(char[14]);       /*declaration of functions*/
void PrintData(int);
char data[100];               /*array of bytes*/
void main()
{
    int bytes,i;
    char filename[14];
    system("cls");
    printf("\nLoad data from disc file\n");
    printf("\nEnter name of disc file > ");
    scanf("%s",filename);
    bytes = DiscLoad(filename);          /*Call function DiscLoad */
```

```
       PrintData(bytes);
    }
int DiscLoad(char filename[14])
{
    int fd, bytes = 0;
    fd = open(filename,S_IREAD);
    if(fd==-1)
        printf("\n Cannot open file: %s",filename);
    else
    {
        read(fd,data,(bytes = filelength(fd)));
        printf("\n%d bytes loaded from %s\n",bytes,filename);
    }
    close(fd);
    return bytes; /*The number of bytes read from file will be passed
        back to main*/
}
void PrintData(int bytes)
{
    int i;
    for(i = 0; i < bytes; i++) /*Print data*/
    printf("\n%2d %4X",i + 1,data[i]);
}
```

Listing 7.5.11 *(cont.)*

7.5.12 Exercise – alternative load data from a disc file

This is an alternative disc load listing which uses command line input. Note the following points:

(i) Command line arguments; **int argc and char *argv[]** allow data required by the program to be input using strings of characters, separated by spaces, following the program name. **argc** stores the number of strings, the program name counts as the first string. ***argv** is an address pointer to an array. A table is created during program run-time (Figure 7.9), which holds the address of each command line string. Each string is then stored consecutively in memory.
(ii) **argv[1]**, the address of the data file name, is passed to function DiscLoad() from main().

Example (a) int argc and char *argv[]

When in directory EXERCISE the program is executed by:

typing in **discld2** ⟨*datafile*⟩

The program produces a table, Figure 7.9, which has the address of each

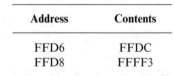

Address	Contents
FFD6	FFDC
FFD8	FFFF3

Figure 7.9 Addresses of command line strings

	String array	
argv[]	**Address**	**String**
[0]	FFDC	c:\exercise\diskld2.exe
[1]	FFF3	*datafile*

Figure 7.10 Strings stored at the address given in the contents of Figure 7.9

string. A further table which stores the strings, Figure 7.10, is then produced.

```
/*discld2.c load data from a disc file. Input file name on command
   line */
#include <stdio.h>              /*required for printf() and scanf() */
#include <stdlib.h>             /*required for system()*/
#include <io.h>                 /*required for open() and read() */
#include <sys\stat.h>           /* to define S_IREAD */
int DiscLoad(char filename[14]); /*declaration of functions*/
void PrintData(int);
char data[100];                 /*array of bytes*/
void main(int argc, char *argv[])
{
    int bytes,i;
    if (argc<2)   /*Checks to see if data file name has been entered*/
    {
        printf("\nEnter file name after discld2 \n");
        exit(1);
    }
    system("cls");
    printf("\nLoad data from disc file\n");
    bytes=DiscLoad(argv[1]);     /*Call function DiscLoad */
    PrintData(bytes);
}
int DiscLoad(char filename[14])
{
    int fd, bytes=0;
    fd=open(filename,S_IREAD);
    if(fd==-1)
        printf("\n Cannot open file: %s",filename);
    else
    {
        read(fd,data,(bytes=filelength(fd)));
        printf("\n%d bytes loaded from %s\n",bytes,filename);
    }
    close(fd);
```

Listing 7.5.12 discld2.c

```
    return bytes;        /*The number of bytes read from the file will be
        passed back to main*/
}
void PrintData(int bytes)
{
    int i;
    for(i = 0; i < bytes; i++)        /*Print data*/
        printf("\n%2d %4X",i + 1,data[i]);
}
```

Listing 7.5.12   *(cont.)*

7.5.13   Exercise – temperature conversion

One method of offering program users a number of options is to present them with a *menu* so that a given option can be selected. The following program provides one way of achieving this. The listing for this exercise is derived from the structure chart of Figure 6.6 which is repeated here as Figure 7.11 for convenience. Note the following points:

(i)   On the statement **menu = toupper(getch());** The program first waits for a character to be input from the keyboard, if it is not *upper* case it will convert it to upper case and then store it in the menu variable.

(ii)   Functions **switch()**, **case** and **break** are used together for the selection of an action according to the letter stored in menu. **break** must be used after each selection except the last, otherwise all the selections will be implemented to the end of the **switch** function.

(iii)   The Kelvin() and Fahrenheit() functions in this listing are *blank stubs*. Blank stubs are a convenient way of testing a **menu** when there are many functions to be written. It makes debugging much

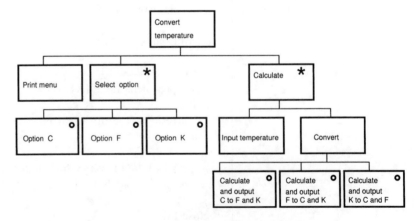

Figure 7.11   Repeat of JSP chart from Chapter 6

easier if the menu is written with blank stubs, and then one function written and tested at a time.

(iv) // is an alternative one line comment.

```c
/*tempconv.c   Temperature Scale Converter */
#include <stdio.h>       /*Required for the getch() function*/
#include <string.h>      /*Required for the toupper() string function*/
void Celsius(float);     /*Convert C to F and K*/
void Fahrenheit(float);  /*Convert F to C and K*/
void Kelvin(float);      /*Convert K to C and F*/
int CalcTemp(char);
void main()
{
    char menu ='X';
    system("cls");
  /* - - - - - - - - - - Print menu - - - - - - - - - - */
    printf("\n\n\n\n\            Temperature Scale Conversion\n\n");
    printf("\n      Enter C for Celsius to Fahrenheit and Kelvin");
    printf("\n            F for Fahrenheit to Celsius and Kelvin");
    printf("\n            K for Kelvin to Celsius and Fahrenheit");
    printf("\n                              Q for quit\n");
  /* - - - - - - - - - - Select Option - - - - - - - - - - */
    while(menu != 'C' & menu != 'F' & menu != 'K') /*Iteration
                                   until C, F or K selected*/
    {
        menu = toupper(getch());   /*get character from
            keyboard and change to upper case if necessary*/
        if(menu =='Q')
        exit(1);
    }
    while(CalcTemp(menu) == 1);
}
int CalcTemp(char menu)
{
    float temp;
    int r = 1;
    system("cls");
    printf("\nEnter %c temperature and press Enter...",menu);
    scanf("%f",&temp);
    switch(menu)             /*Select the function*/
    {
        case 'C'             :Celsius(temp);
                             break;
        case 'F'             :Fahrenheit(temp);
                             break;
        case 'K'             :Kelvin(temp);
    }
    printf("\n\n Press Q to Quit, any other key to continue\n");
```

Listing 7.5.13 tempconv.c

```
                    if (toupper(getch()) =='Q')
                            r = 0;
                    return r;
            }
            void Celsius(float temp)
            {
                    printf("\n\n %.2føC = %.2føF and %.2fK\n",temp,
                            temp*9/5 + 32, temp + 273);
            }
            void Fahrenheit(float temp)
            {
                    //Blank Stub
            }
            void Kelvin(float temp)
            {
                    //Blank stub
            }
```

Listing 7.5.13   *(cont.)*

7.5.14   Exercise – writing functions

Write the Fahrenheit() and Kelvin() functions.

7.6   Selected answers

1   Answer 7.5.1 A   A marathon is 4.218597e + 01 kilometres
2   Answer 7.5.1 B   A marathon is 42.19 kilometres
3   Answer 7.5.6 B   Listing 7.6.1

```c
/*square5.c gives the square of 5 numbers */
#include < stdio.h >
void main()
{
    int number, i;
    printf("\033[2J");
    for(i = 1; i < 6; i++)
    {
        printf("Enter a whole number < 180 ");
        scanf("%d",&number);
        printf("\nThe square of %3d = %3d\n\n",
                                        number,number*number);
    }
}
```

Listing 7.6.1   square5.c

Part Three
Interfacing Exercises

8 Serial interfacing

8.1 Serial data transmission

8.2 Serial interfacing hardware

8.3 Serial data exercises

8.4 Questions

WARNING **The remaining chapters in this book all contain practical exercises which involve making connections to a computer. It is essential that any circuits connected to a computer are first checked by a competent person. The connections and information are given in good faith, but the author cannot be held responsible for damage to equipment, and, although unlikely, injury to any person carrying out these exercises.**

This chapter introduces *serial data transmission* and simple exercises using the *comm. port*.

8.1 Serial data transmission

In serial data transmission, the **bits** which form the character codes are sent one after the other along a single conductor with a ground return. Personal computers (PCs) often have two communications ports (generally known as comm. ports). These ports use asynchronous serial data transmission for sending and receiving ASCII code. The protocol is known as the RS232C standard[1].

Figure 8.2 shows the signal when character 'R' is transmitted. Each character is preceded by a **start** bit (logic 0) and terminated with a **stop** bit (logic 1). There may also be a **parity**[2] check bit added before the stop bit. The stop bit[3] may be equal in length to 1, 1.5 or 2 normal bits.

The number of logic states per second is called the **baud** rate. In a two-state system the baud rate is equal to the number of *bits per second*.

Character	Parity bit	ASCII code
A	0	100 0001
a	1	110 0001
B	0	100 0010
b	1	110 0010
C	1	100 0011
c	0	110 0011

Figure 8.1 ASCII code with even 1s parity

[1] While the term RS232 is still commonly used, it was in fact renamed EIA-232-D in 1987. EIA stands for Electronic Industries Association (USA). The D version of this protocol brings the specification into line with CCITT V.24, V.28 and ISO2110.

[2] Adding a parity bit is a simple form of error checking. A single bit is added to make the number of 1s or the number of 0s odd or even, see Figure 8.1. A single error will change the number of 1s or 0s from odd to even, or vice versa, and hence the error can be detected.

[3] The variable length stop bit was required to cater for some relatively slow mechanical systems.

Bit number	Start	0	1	2	3	4	5	6	Parity	Stop
Bit sequence	0	0	1	0	0	1	0	1	1	1

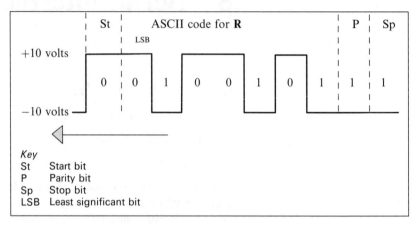

Figure 8.2   RS232 signal for letter 'R'

Figure 8.3   Transmission of a string of characters

When transferring data between two machines, or between a machine and a peripheral, both machines must be set to the same mode[4] so that the receiving clock runs at the same frequency as the transmitting clock, during transfer of a character. The system is *asynchronous* because the minimum number of characters per second is determined by the speed of the sender; that is, the sender can pause for as long as he likes between characters. During any pauses the line will be at logic state 1[5], hence the reason for a logic 0 start bit.

One of the most common ways of transmitting bits in an asynchronous data system is shown in Figure 8.2, where a logic 0 is represented by a voltage greater than +3 volts (typically +10 volts) and a logic 1 is represented by a voltage less than −3 volts (typically −10 volts). 0 V incoming indicates a disconnected line or system not working. Character **R** in 7-bit ASCII code is **101 0010** which is **52 hex**. The LSB of the code, preceded by a logic 0 (start bit), is sent first. The bit sequence is ended with an optional parity and finally a stop bit. Figure 8.3 shows the code for a string of serial characters.

[4] *Mode* is the term used to indicate how the receiver/transmitter chip has been programmed.
[5] This is known as the quiescent state. Logic states may also be referred to in teleprinter terms; that is, logic 1 = **mark** and logic 0 = **space**.

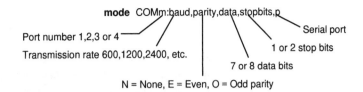

mode COMm:baud,parity,data,stopbits,p

Port number 1,2,3 or 4

Transmission rate 600,1200,2400, etc.

N = None, E = Even, O = Odd parity

7 or 8 data bits

1 or 2 stop bits

Serial port

Example   Type > mode com1:9600,n,8,1,p.

Figure 8.4   MS DOS mode command

The mode of the receiver/transmitter chip may be programmed using one of the following methods:

(i)   A software package.
(ii) The MS-DOS **mode** command, Figure 8.4.
(iii) An instruction in a C program.

8.2 Serial interfacing hardware

Special ICs known as *universal asynchronous receiver/transmitters* (UARTs)[6] convert parallel (TTL) data from the microprocessor data bus to serial (RS232) data format and vice versa. These devices can be considered as having two internal sections, a parallel to serial converter called the transmitter and a serial to parallel converter called the receiver. The transmitter inserts the start, stop and parity bits. The receiver checks the format and parity of the received data. The receiver and transmitter can operate simultaneously, such transmissions are called *full duplex*[7].

The transmit and receive data rates are controlled by an internal or external clock running at some multiple of the data rate. An internal status register, which stores receive, transmit and error states, can be read under program control.

The standard connector is a **25-pin D-type** (male) connector. In some cases, however, a 9-pin connector, which accommodates the most commonly used control lines, is used. The pin-assignment of the 25-way connector is shown in Figure 8.5. Those pins which are most widely used are in **bold type**.

Many interconnecting cables require **pin 2** to be interchanged with **pin 3** and **pin 4** to be interchanged with **pin 5**. Figure 8.6 shows a typical cable arrangement. In general manufacturers of peripherals either give the cable connections or provide a suitable cable.

8.3 Serial data exercises

The comm. port address should be checked for the machine being used. Typical PC addresses for both sending and receiving data are:

[6] UARTs are also known as asynchronous communications interface adapters (ACIAs), or asynchronous communications elements (ACEs).
[7] Transmission in one direction only is known as *simplex*. Transmission in both directions, but not at the same time, is called *half duplex*.

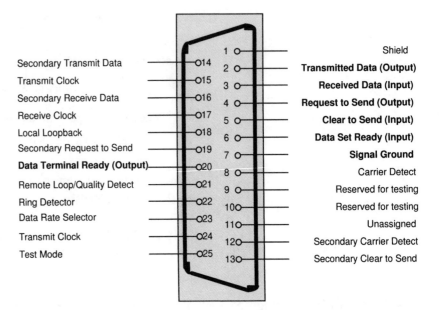

Figure 8.5   Comm. port pin assignment

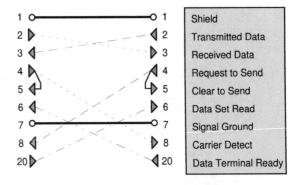

Figure 8.6   Typical RS232

Comm. 1   3F8 hex
Comm. 2   2F8 hex

8.3.1   Exercise – serial loop-back test

Send a character from the Transmitted Data (TD) pin (pin 2) and receive the character on the Received Data (RD) pin (pin 3) of the same port. Only one computer is required for this test. The TD pin 2 is connected to the RD pin 3 on the same port.

There are several connection arrangements available from equipment suppliers. The one illustrated in Figure 8.7, together with an easily

Figure 8.7 Equipment for Exercise 8.3.1

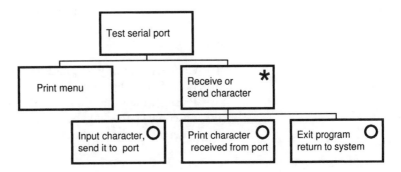

Figure 8.8 Structure chart for Exercise 8.3.1

obtainable 25-way cable, is suitable for exercises both in this chapter and in Chapter 12.

A structure chart for the software is shown in Figure 8.8.

Listing 8.3.1 serial1.c

```
/*serial1.c  Serial port Test */
#include < stdio.h >
#include < conio.h >
int Address = 0x3f8; /*Address of Comm 1,change to 0x2f8 if using
    Comm 2 */
void main()
{
    printf("\033[2J");        /*Clears the screen*/
    printf("\n Data transfer via the serial port");
    printf("\n R to receive data");
    printf("\n S to send data");
    printf("\n Q to quit\n");
    while (1)
    {
        switch(toupper(getch()))
        {
        case 'S' :    printf("\n Send a Character from the keyboard ");
                      outp(Address,getche());
```

```
                              printf("\nS, R, Q?");
                              break;
             case 'R' :       printf("\n Character received > %c",inp(Address));
                              printf("\nS, R, Q?");
                              break;
             case 'Q' :       exit(1);
             }
             fflush(stdin);

       }
}
```

Listing 8.3.1   *(cont.)*

Testing 8.3.1

(i)   Connect comm. port pin 2 to pin 3.
(ii)   Press S and then a character.
(iii)   Press R: the same character should be received on the screen.
(iv)   Disconnect the link between pins 2 and 3. When R is pressed, a different character should be received.

8.3.2   Exercise – investigation of comm. port signals

This exercise requires the use of a storage oscilloscope.

(i)   Connect the storage CRO **input** to the pin 2–pin 3 link and CRO **ground** to pin 7 of the comm. port connector.
(ii)   Set the storage CRO to trigger when a character is sent. The **input** should be on DC, and the **sensitivity** to 5 volts/div.
(iii)   Use the program developed for Exercise 8.3.1 to output a character.
(iv)   Adjust the CRO timebase so that a complete character of 10 bits is displayed. The timebase setting will depend on the baud rate.
(v)   Copy at least six waveforms of upper and lower case characters. Use different baud rates, data bits, stop bits and parity.
(vi)   Note the voltage of the logic 1 and logic 0 signals.
(vii)   Measure the period of each bit and the period of the character. Relate this to the baud rate of transmission.
(viii)   Decipher the waveforms into binary and hence show that they are the ASCII codes of the keys pressed.

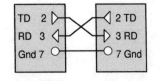

Figure 8.9   Connections for Exercise 8.3.3

8.3.3   Exercise – communication between two computers

The aim of this exercise is to transfer characters between two computers. Hence this exercise requires a second computer. Connect the comm. ports of the two computers together as shown in Figure 8.9. Pin 2 of one computer must be connected to pin 3 of the other.

(i) Make sure that both computers are running in the same **mode**.
(ii) Run the program for Exercise 8.3.1 on both computers.
(iii) Send a character from one machine and receive it on the other. The system should work in both directions (half duplex).
(iv) Use the MS-DOS **mode** command to change mode on both machines. Investigate what happens if the machines are running at different Baud rates, or if they have a different number of data bits.

8.3.4 Exercise – text transmission

Develop the program (Listing 8.3.1) so that a string of say 20 characters can be sent down the link. The main problem with sending text via the comm. port is that some way of indicating to the sending computer that a character has been read is necessary. This can be achieved by using handshaking with the control lines or if it is desired to keep to a three-wire system, an acknowledge character may be sent by the receiver when a character is read. Alternatively text can be sent in packets of a prescribed number of characters from a file.

8.4 Questions

1 Why is each character preceded by a start bit?
2 Give two advantages of using balanced voltages for the transmission of the logic states, rather than using (TTL) 5 and 0 volts.
3 Which logic state is transmitted between characters?
4 How long does it take to send a 7-bit character plus a parity check bit at a transmission rate of 1000 bauds?
5 In a three-wire system with just pins 2, 3 and 7 interconnected, how does the receiving device know if the sending device is not connected?

9 Parallel interfacing

9.1 The Intel 82C55A PPI

9.2 Stepper motor exercises

The exercises described in Chapters 9, 10 and 11 use a card in the PC containing an Intel 8255 programmable parallel interface (PPI) IC. Information concerning the operation of the 8255 PPI has been obtained from the Intel Data Sheet and printed here by permission of Intel Corporation (UK) Ltd.

The hardware used in these exercises is described in Chapter 14. An LED box is illustrated in Figure 9.16, at the end of this chapter.

Parallel data transfer is a system whereby each bit of a binary word is transmitted along its own conductor. Thus 16-bit words require 16 conductors. An additional conductor is required as a *common* or *ground* return. In some cables, to reduce interference from pulses travelling on adjacent conductors, each conductor forms a twisted pair with a ground conductor.

9.1 The Intel 82C55A PPI

Cards containing the 8255 PPI are available from a number of suppliers. This card is a worthwhile addition to a PC used for interfacing purposes, as it is far easier to use than the serial (comm.) port, and has many more facilities than the parallel printer port.

Unfortunately there are no standard connections or addresses for PPI cards, so both pin numbers and addresses given are for example only. Space has been allowed in the tables of Figures 9.1 and 9.2 for addresses and pin numbers of the user's board to be inserted. The relevant information should be supplied with the card. Addresses used in programs are also for example only and may have to be changed. The PPI requires a sequence of four addresses. The lowest address is called the **base** address. The other three addresses are then referred to as **base + 1**, **base + 2** and **base + 3**. Some form of address selection is usually provided on the card. Care must be taken that the address selected is not used by another application, such as a network interface.

The PPI has three 8-bit *ports* which may be configured in several ways as described below. There are three modes of operation (mode 0, mode 1 and mode 2). An 8-bit word written to the *control register* of the PPI configures the mode and data direction of each port. This control word is included in the program before any other instructions.

Output voltages are normal TTL (0 V for logic 0 and 5 V for logic 1).

Port	Address (hex)	Address (hex)
	Example	Actual
A	300	
B	301	
C	302	
Control	303	

Figure 9.1 Typical PPI addresses

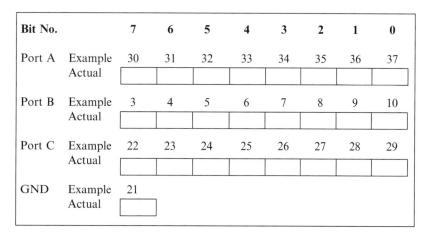

Bit No.		7	6	5	4	3	2	1	0
Port A	Example	30	31	32	33	34	35	36	37
	Actual								
Port B	Example	3	4	5	6	7	8	9	10
	Actual								
Port C	Example	22	23	24	25	26	27	28	29
	Actual								
GND	Example	21							
	Actual								

Figure 9.2 Typical PPI card pin numbers

The exercises use the PPI in mode 0. I have included some details of mode 1 operation, as an example of the handshaking technique of data transfer. Mode 2, which uses half duplex operation on port A, will not be described.

Figure 9.1 is a table showing typical hexadecimal addresses of a parallel I/O board using an 8255 PPI.

Figure 9.2 is a table of typical pin numbers on a 37-way connector for the 24 bits plus ground. In some cases a 5 volt supply is also available, but for experiments, it is better to use an external supply. Make sure all the common grounds are connected!

9.1.1 PPI mode 0 (basic input/output)

This mode provides simple input and output operations for ports A, B and C. Port C is divided into two 4-bit ports (bits 0 to 3 and bits 4 to 7). Other features are:

(i)   All ports are set to input after reset.
(ii) The outputs are latched.
(iii) Ports are cleared when the PPI control register is written to.

Control word for mode 0

Bit No.	7	6	5	4	3	2	1	0
Code	1	0	0	A	CH	0	B	CL

A = port A   A = 0 for output, 1 for input
B = port B   B = 0 for output, 1 for input
CL = port C bits 0 to 3   CL = 0 for output, 1 for input
CH = port C bits 4 to 7   CH = 0 for output, 1 for input

Figure 9.3 Mode 0 control word

Example of control word for mode 0

Configure the PPI to input from port A, output to port B and input from port C.

> Bit 0 = 1 (replace CL with 1)
> Bit 1 = 0 (replace B with 0)
> Bit 3 = 1 (replace CH with 1)
> Bit 4 = 1 (replace A with 1)

Control word 1 0 0 1 1 0 0 1 = 99 Hex

9.1.2   Exercise – number output mode 0

The aim of this exercise is to show that the output system is working correctly by sending binary numbers to **port B** of the PPI. Both a C

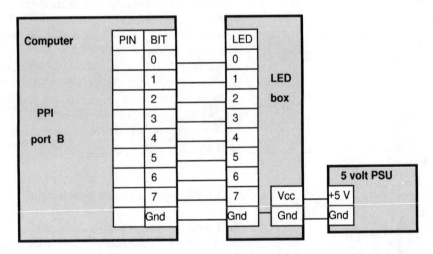

Figure 9.4   Mode 0 hardware output test

program and the hardware connections, Figure 9.4, are provided.

Software structure for mode 0 output test

> Configure the PPI,   mode 0
> ports A and C to input data,
> port B to output data.
>
> Print instructions
> while not end
> {

Input 2 hex digits from keyboard.
Output binary number to port B

}
exit

```
/*output.c   Output data to port B. Port B should be connected to an
   LED box.*/
#include < dos.h >
#include < stdio.h >        /*Required for the scanf() function*/
int Output();               /*Name for function used in the program*/
int Control = 0x303;        /*Address of control register*/
int B_Address = 0x301;      /*Base + 1 address*/
int config = 0x99;          /*99 Hex configures the port as follows
                Port A to input
                Port B to output
                Port CL to input
                Port CH to input */
void main()
{
   int menu;                /*Define internal variable*/
   outp(Control,config);    /*Configure PPI*/
   printf("\n\n\n\tDATA OUTPUT from PORT B");
   printf("\n\n\tPress NON-HEX character to quit");
   while (Output());        /*Continue until output = 0*/
   exit(1);
}
int Output()
{
   int data,x;
   printf("\n\n\t Enter a Hex number, press ENTER ");
   fflush(stdin);           /*flush the keyboard buffer*/
   x = scanf("%2X",
      &data);               /*Get the data from the keyboard*/
   outp(B_Address,data);    /*Send the data to the port*/
   return x;                /*x is 0 for non-hex number*/
}
```

Listing 9.1.2   output.c

9.1.3   Exercise – input test mode 0

The aim of this exercise is to test the input system. The program provided
scans port A and shows the logic position of switches connected to Port
A. Figure 9.5 provides the connections to the PPI required for this
exercise.

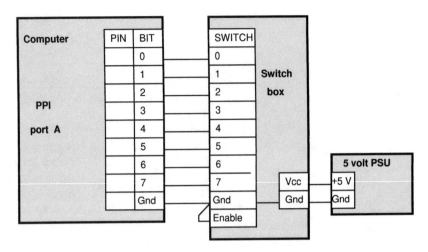

Figure 9.5　Mode 0 hardware input test

Software structure for PPI mode 0, input test

> configure PPI A input, B and C output
> print　　instructions and bit heading
> while (key is not pressed)
> 　　　　input from port A and print result on screen
> exit

```
/*input.c   Input data from parallel port A. Port A connected to a
      switch box.*/
#include <dos.h>
#include <stdio.h>
int Input();
int A_Address = 0x300;          /*Address of Port A*/
int Control = 0x303;            /*Control Register address*/
int Config = 0x99;              /*Configuration
                                    Port A to input
                                    Port B to output
                                    Port CL to input
                                    Port CH to input */
void main()
{
    outp(Control,Config);       /*Configure the PPI*/
    clrscr();
    printf("\n\n\n\t DATA INPUT from Port A");
    printf("\n\nPress any key to Quit");
    printf("\033[15;5H Bit 7 6 5 4 3 2 1 0");
    printf("\033[16;5H State ");
    while(!Input());            /*Continue until Input() function
                                            outputs a 1*/

    exit(1);
```

```
}
int Input()
{
    int data,i;

    data = inp(A_Address);         /*Input data from port B*/
    printf("\033[16;12H");         /*Position cursor*/
    for(i = 7; i>-1; i--)
        printf(" %1x ",(data > >i)&1);     /*shifts data i bits and then
                                                   AND it with 1*/

    printf(" = %2x",data);
    return kbhit();
}
```

Listing 9.1.3   input.c

Figure 9.6 is a trace table of the boxed-in segment of Listing 9.1.3. This is to show how the digital position of the switches connected to port A are reproduced on the screen.

```
data = inp(A_Address);         /*Input data from port B*/
printf("\033[16;12H");         /*Position cursor*/
for(i = 7; i>-1; i--)
    printf(" %1x ",(data >> i)&1);
                               /*shifts data i bits and then AND it with 1*/
```

	i	Binary data	Screen O/P 76543210	Comment
data	7	1100 0101		Number from switches
data >> i		xxxxxxx1		Shift data to the right
(data >> i)&1		1		Bitwise AND with 1
printf("1x",(data >> i)&1)			1	Print 1 hex digit
data >> i	6	xxxxxx11		Repeat for i = 6
(data >> i)&1		1		
printf("1x",(data >> i)&1)			1	
data >> i	5	xxxxx110		Repeat for i = 5
(data >> i)&1		0		
printf("1x",(data >> i)&1)			0	
data >> i	4	xxx1100		Repeat for i = 4
(data >> i)&1		0		
printf("1x",(data >> i)&1)			0	
Iteration continues until i = 0				

Figure 9.6   Trace table for boxed-in segment of Listing 9.1.3

9.1.4   PPI mode 1, strobed input/output

The PPI in mode 1 provides a means of transferring data to/from port A or port B in conjunction with strobes or 'handshaking' signals. The specific features are:

  (i) Two 8-bit ports (A and B).
 (ii) Port C is used for control of A and B.
(iii) The two ports can be input or output.
 (iv) Inputs and outputs are latched.
  (v) Interrupt facility available on C0 and C3.

Control word for mode 0

Bit No.	7	6	5	4	3	2	1	0
Code	1	0	1	A	A	1	B	B

A = port A   A = 0 for output, 1 for input
B = port B   B = 0 for output, 1 for input

Figure 9.7   Mode 1 control word

Example of control words for mode 1
Program port A for input and B for output. Control word = 10**11**1**00** = BC hex.

Handshaking
In mode 1, port C is used for handshaking signals to facilitate data transfer. Handshaking is a protocol where the data originator signals that data is ready, and the data receiver signals an acknowledgement. The output control handshaking signals are shown in table form in Figure 9.8 and in timing diagram form in Figure 9.9.

9.1.5   Exercise – PPI mode 1, output test

Output	Data	Label	Comment/Action
Port A	Port B		
C7	C1	OBF	This OUTPUT signal goes LOW when outgoing data has been written to the port. It goes HIGH when ACK goes LOW.
C6	C2	ACK	The peripheral applies a LOW to this terminal when it has accepted data.

OBF = Output buffer full
ACK = Acknowledge

Figure 9.8   Mode 1 output handshaking signals

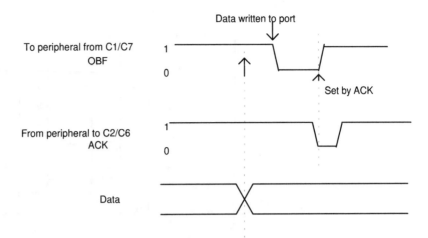

Figure 9.9 Mode 1 output handshaking timing diagram

Mode 1 output test: structure chart and operation
Figure 9.11 is the structure chart for this exercise. The hardware is shown in Figure 9.10. Note a switch box and a second LED box are required.

When the program is executed the events are as follows:

(i)   Request a hexadecimal number from the keyboard.
(ii) If the control switch on C2 is at logic 1, the program will then display **Waiting for a logic 0 on C2**.
(iii) When a logic 0 is applied to C2, data will be sent to port B, the control LED on C1 will go **ON**.
(iv) The program will then display **Waiting for a logic 1 on C2**.
(v)   When the switch on C2 is moved to logic 1, the control LED will go **OFF**.
(vi) Repeat from (i).

```
/*outmode1.c   Output B with handshaking signals. Port B should be
connected to an LED box. An LED should also be connected to C1
and a logic switch to C2*/
#include < dos.h >
#include < stdio.h >          /*Required for the scanf() function*/
int Output();                 /*Name for function used in the program*/
int Control = 0x303;          /*Address of control register*/
int B_Address = 0x301;        /*Base + 1 address*/
int C_Address = 0x302;        /*Base + 2 address*/
int config = 0xBC;            /*BC configures the port as follows
                                    Port A to input
                                    Port B to output */

void main()
{
```

Listing 9.1.5 outmode1.c

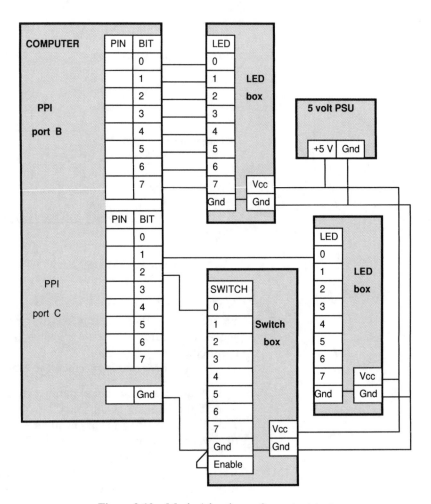

Figure 9.10   Mode 1 hardware for output test

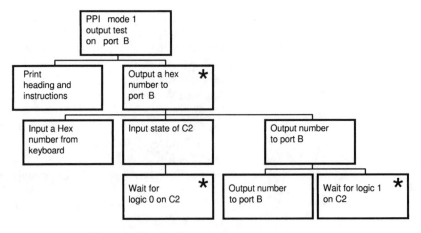

Figure 9.11   Mode 1 output test structure chart

```
    int menu;                    /*Define integer variable*/
    clrscr();
    outp(Control,config);        /*Configure PPI*/
    printf("\n\n\n\tDATA OUTPUT from PORT B");
    printf("\n\n\tPress NON-HEX character to quit");
    printf("\n\nInput a Logic 0 on C2");
    while (Output());            /*Continue until output = 0*/
    exit(1);
}
int Output()
{
    int data,x,k = 2;
    printf("\033[16;1H Enter a Hex number, press ENTER ");
    fflush(stdin);               /*flush the keyboard buffer*/
    x = scanf("%2X",&data);      /*Get the data from the keyboard*/
    do
    {
        outp(B_Address,data);    /*Send the data to the port*/
        k = inp(C_Address) & 2;
        printf("\033[18;1H Data sent Input Logic 1 pulse on C2 to
                                            Acknowledge ");

    }
        while(k != 0);
        printf("\033[18;1H C1 L.E.D OFF and ON when C2 returned
                                            to Logic 0 ");

        printf("\033[16;1H            ");
        return x;                /*x is 0 for non-hex number*/
}
```

Listing 9.1.5 *(cont.)*

9.1.6 Exercise – mode 1 input test

The input handshaking signals are shown in table form in Figure 9.12 and in timing diagram form in Figure 9.13.

Input	Data	Label	Comment/Action
Port A	Port B		
C4	C2	STB	A LOW on this INPUT from a peripheral loads data into the input register.
C5	C1	IBF	A HIGH on this OUTPUT acknowledges that data has been loaded into the input register. Goes LOW when data has been read.

STB = Strobe input
IBF = Input buffer full

Figure 9.12 Mode 1 input handshaking signals

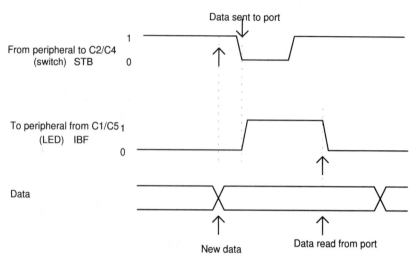

Figure 9.13   Mode 1 input handshaking timing diagram

The hardware connections for this exercise are similar to those for the mode 1 output test, except for the following:

(i)   The connection to C1 is moved to C5.
(ii)   The connection to C2 is moved to C4.
(iii)   A switch box is connected to port A.

The software for this exercise is given in Listing 9.1.6. The operating procedure is given in the listing. Basically a logic 0 pulse is required on C4 before the data is input from port A.

9.2   Stepper motor exercises

This section contains three exercises which involve the development of programs to control the speed and direction of a stepper motor. The motor, which is connected to port B, is controlled by binary switches connected to port A

9.2.1   Exercise – stepper motor control

(i)   Develop software which will control a stepper motor, giving it two clockwise speeds, two anticlockwise speeds and stop. See the structure chart of Figure 9.14.
(ii)   Connect up the hardware as shown in Figure 9.15.
(iii)   Adjust the delays in the program so that the motor runs fast and slow smoothly. Note the first delay for each sequence is made shorter to allow for computer time when looping back. If the code for motor rotation is sent too quickly the motor will vibrate.

```
/*inmode1.c   Mode 1 test program input A with handshaking signals*/
/*Input data from Port A. Port A should be connected to a SWITCH box.*/
/* An LED should be connected to C5 and a logic switch to C4*/
#include < dos.h >
#include < stdio.h >              /*Required for the scanf() function*/
int Input();                      /*Name for function used in the program*/
int Control = 0x303;              /*Address of control register*/
int B_Address = 0x301;           /*Base + 1 address*/
int A_Address = 0x300;           /*Base address*/
int C_Address = 0x302;           /*Base address + 2*/
int config = 0xBC;               /*BC configures the port as follows
                                 Port A to input
                                 Port B to output
                                 Port C4 Input Handshake
                                 Port C5 Output Handshake */
void main()
{
   clrscr();
   outp(Control,config);         /*Configure PPI*/
   printf("\n\n\n\tDATA INPUT from PORT A");
   printf("\n\n\tPress ENTER to input data any other key to quit");
   printf("\033[12;1HEnter Binary Number on PORT A ");
   printf("\nApply logic 0 pulse on C4........LED on C5 should go ON");
   printf("\nPress ENTER to input data");
   printf("\nfrom PORT A........................LED on C5 should go OFF");
   while (Input() );             /*Continue until 0 returned*/
   exit(1);
}
int Input()
{
   int k,r = 1;
   if (getch() == 13)
      printf("\033[18;1H Data: %0X",inp(A_Address));
   else r = 0;
   return r;
}
```

Listing 9.1.6   inmode1.c

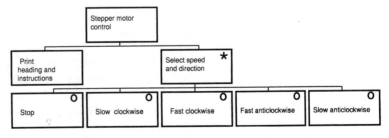

Figure 9.14   Stepper motor control structure chart

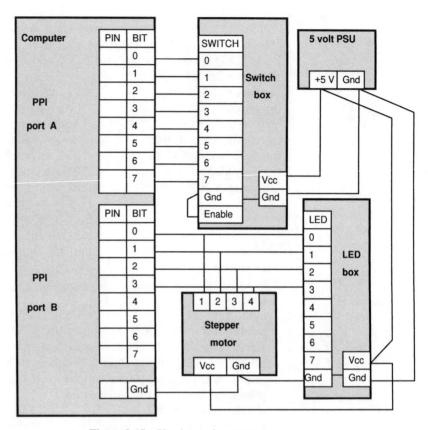

Figure 9.15   Hardware for stepper motor control

Software structure for Exercise 9.2.1

Initialise PPI mode 0, port A for input and port B for output.
Print instructions

All switches at logic 0 to stop motor.
Switches to logic 1 as shown in the table below.

Switch (to logic 1)	Mode	Denary value
	stop	0
0	clockwise slow	1
1	clockwise fast	2
2	anticlockwise fast	4
3	anticlockwise slow	8

while (not end)
{

    input   mode from port A
    output   number sequence for one rotation of the stepper
            motor. The sequence of numbers to rotate the
            motor clockwise is 3, 6, 12, 9

}
exit

```
/*motor.c  Stepper motor control program. Speed and direction of motor
input from port A. Port A0 to A3 connected to a switch box. Number
sequence to control motor output to port B. Port B0 to B3 connected to an
LED box and motor.*/
#include < dos.h >
#include < stdio.h >
int A_Address = 0x300;   /*Port A address*/
int B_Address = 0x301;   /*Port B address*/
int Control = 0x303;     /*Control address*/
int Config = 0x99;       /*Configuration, Port A input, Port B output*/
int Input();
void Rotate(int,int);
int clockwise = 0;
int anticlock = 1;
int slow = 1000;         /*These two speeds may be adjusted according to */
int fast = 100 ;         /*the speed of the computer. The higher the */
                         /*number the slower the motor*/
void main()
{
    outp(Control,Config);
    clrscr();
    printf("\n\n\n\t\tSTEPPER MOTOR CONTROL");
    printf("\n\n\tControl the motor from the switch box");
    printf("\n\tIf all switches are at logic 0 ");
    printf("the motor will stop");
    printf("\n\tHit any key to quit program");
    printf("\n\n\t\tSWITCH MODE");
    printf("\n\t\t 0 slow clockwise");
    printf("\n\t\t 1 fast clockwise");
    printf("\n\t\t 2 fast anticlockwise");
    printf("\n\t\t 3 slow anticlockwise");
    while(!Input());
    exit(1);
}
int Input()
{
    printf("%i",inp(A_Address)) ;
    switch(inp(A_Address) & 0x0F)
    {
        case 1 :        Rotate(slow,clockwise);
                        break;
        case 2 :        Rotate(fast,clockwise);
                        break;
        case 4 :        Rotate(fast,anticlock);
                        break;
        case 8 :        Rotate(slow,anticlock);
                        break;
```

Listing 9.2.1   motor.c

```
          default :                printf("\033[20;10HMotor stopped");
    }
    return kbhit();
}
void Rotate(int speed, int direction)
{
    int i;
    int data[2][4] = {3,6,12,9,        /*Code for rotate clockwise*/
                      9,12,6,3};       /*Code for rotate anti clockwise*/
    delay(speed * 5/10);
    printf("\033[20;10H              ");
    for(i = 0; i < 4; i++)
    {
        outp(B_Address,data[direction][i]);   /*Send code to motor*/
        delay(speed);
    }
}
```

Listing 9.2.1   (*cont.*)

9.2.2   Exercise – three-speed motor control

Modify the software of Exercise 9.2.1 to provide for slow, medium and fast speeds of the motor in each direction.

9.2.3   Exercise – control of two stepper motors

Add an additional stepper motor to the unused output pins of port B and modify the software to control two stepper motors from the one set of switches.

Figure 9.16   LED box

10 Digital to analogue parallel interfacing

Chapters 10 and 11 use the PPI port, introduced in Chapter 9, to implement digital to analogue conversion in this chapter, and analogue to digital conversion in Chapter 11.

10.1 Digital to analogue conversion

A digital to analogue converter (D to A, or DAC) produces an output voltage which is proportional to an applied binary number. There are many ICs available which use different methods to implement this conversion. To illustrate the process, a 4-bit **R-2R** ladder method, as shown in Figure 10.1, will be described here.

Referring to Figure 10.1, Vs is a reference voltage, usually derived from the DC supply rail, which provides a constant current into the R-2R network. The impedance offered to the source, Vs, by the ladder network is a constant resistance of value R Ω, typically between 1 kΩ and 5 kΩ. Hence the current supplied by Vs must be constant. The position of each *analogue switch* is set according to the binary signal from the *register*. A logic 0 from the register moves the switch to ground position, and a logic 1 moves it to the *op. amp.* input rail.

As a result of the op. amp.'s high gain, there is only a very small PD between its *non-inverting* (+) and the *inverting* (−) input terminals. Consequently the (−) op. amp. input is said to be a *virtual ground*. Hence the current in the network does not change when the analogue switches change position.

Current I from Vs is divided by two at each network node[1]. Hence the current through switches A, B, C, and D will be 0.5I, 0.25I, 0.125I and 0.0625I respectively.

Figure 10.2 shows the relationship of the switch positions, the current through each switch, the current at the op. amp. input, and the output

---

[1] A network *node* is a junction of two or more components.

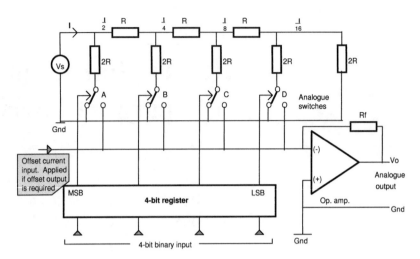

Figure 10.1   R-2R DAC

Switch position	Proportion of current (I) through switches				Current at op. amp. input (+)	Output voltage
A B C D	A	B	C	D	Total I	(I(+)) Rf
0 0 0 0	0.0	0.0	0.0	0.0	0.0	0.0
0 0 0 1	0.0	0.0	0.0	0.0625	0.0625I	−0.625
0 0 1 0	0.0	0.0	0.125	0.0	0.125I	−1.25
0 0 1 1	0.0	0.0	0.125	0.0625	0.1875I	−1.875
0 1 0 0	0.0	0.25	0.0	0.0	0.25I	−2.5
0 1 0 1	0.0	0.25	0.0	0.0625	0.3125I	−3.125
0 1 1 0	0.0	0.25	0.125	0.0	0.375I	−3.75
0 1 1 1	0.0	0.25	0.125	0.0625	0.4375I	−4.375
1 0 0 0	0.5	0.0	0.0	0.0	0.5I	−5.0
1 0 0 1	0.5	0.0	0.0	0.0625	0.5625I	−5.625
1 0 1 0	0.5	0.0	0.125	0.0	0.625I	−6.25
1 0 1 1	0.5	0.0	0.125	0.0625	0.6875I	−6.875
1 1 0 0	0.5	0.25	0.0	0.0	0.75I	−7.5
1 1 0 1	0.5	0.25	0.0	0.0625	0.8125I	−8.125
1 1 1 0	0.5	0.25	0.125	0.0	0.875I	−8.75
1 1 1 1	0.5	0.25	0.125	0.0625	0.9375I	−9.375

Figure 10.2   Table of test voltages

voltage developed across feedback resistor Rf. The calculation of output voltages assumes an Rf of $2\,k\Omega$ and current $I = 5\,mA$.

Figure 10.2 shows that if the reference voltage is positive the output will vary from $0\,V$ to a negative value. The output may be made symmetrical about 0 volts by introducing a bias current equal to $-0.5I$ at the point shown on Figure 10.1.

One important requirement of D to A circuits is linearity. The linearity of the circuit determines how faithfully the analogue signal follows the binary numbers. Ideally the output voltage should decrease by equal steps as the binary input increases as shown in the table of Figure 10.2.

10.2   D to A exercise

The exercises in Chapters 10, 11 and 12 all use a ZN425 which is a DAC/ADC; however, any similar IC may be used. Some modern ICs will require fewer components in the ADC circuits described in Chapters 11 and 12.

10.2.1   Exercise – D to A test

The aim of this exercise is to construct a D to A interface circuit and connect it to the computer PPI port. Both the circuit, Figure 10.3, and the software listing are provided. The hardware and software should be developed and tested separately.

The test arrangement using a power supply with outputs +5, 0, −5, a switch box and a variable voltage supply is shown in Figure 10.4.

Testing the circuit
When possible test the hardware before connecting it to a computer. The test arrangement is shown in Figure 10.5.

To test the DAC interface:

(i)   After carefully checking the circuit, connect the power supply (+5 V, GND, −5 V).
(ii) Connect the input to a set of binary switches.
(iii) Connect the output to a voltmeter or CRO.

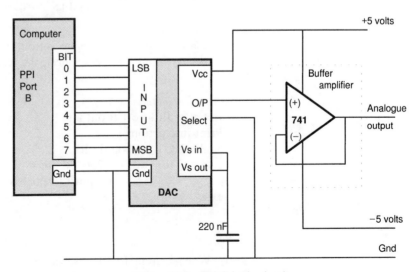

Figure 10.3   DAC logic circuit

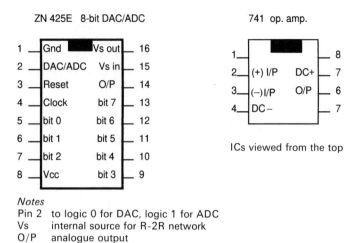

Figure 10.4 IC pin assignment

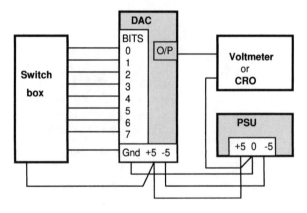

Figure 10.5 DAC test set-up

(iv) Check that the analogue output is directly proportional to the binary input numbers. Check the whole range from 0 to 11111111.

Software structure

Initialise PPI port B output
Print instructions
while (NOT keyboard hit)
  for(i = 0; i < 256; i++)
    output i to port B
exit

Software testing

(i) When Listing 10.2.1 has been successfully compiled. Test the software by connecting an LED box to the PPI port B. Check that when

```
/*dac1.c   The output from this program counts from 0 to 255 in
binary. The output from the DAC should start at 0 volts and decrease
by 255 steps to the maximum negative voltage. Test the software
output with an LED box connected to PPI port B. Finally test with D
to A circuit connected to port B*/
#include < conio.h >              /*for kbhit() function*/
#include < stdio.h >              /*for printf() function*/
#include < dos.h >                 /*for outp() function*/
int B_Address = 0x301;           /* Change if necessary*/
int Control = 0x303;             /*Control address for PPI output*/
int Config = 0x90;                /*PPI configuration*/
void main()
{
    int i;
    outp(Control,Config);         /*Configure PPI*/
    printf("\n\n\tTEST D TO A OUTPUT.");
    printf("\n\n\tHit any key to quit\n");
    while(1)
    {
        for(i = 0; i < 256; i++)
        {

            outp(B_Address,i);
            delay(50);            /*for LED box test only*/
            printf("%i\t",i);     /*for test only*/
            if (kbhit())
                exit(1);
        }
    }
}
```

Listing 10.2.1 dac1.c

the program is executed the output counts up from 0 to binary
11111111.

(ii) Now connect the D to A circuit to the computer and check for
correct operation of the system.

10.3 Waveform generator

The exercises in this section illustrate how a microprocessor can be used
for generating periodic waveforms. The frequency of the waveforms will
be limited by the speed of processing.

10.3.1 Exercise – waveform generator

This exercise demonstrates one of the simpler waveforms which the
computer can generate. A CRO is connected to the output of the circuit

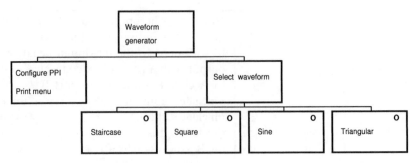

Figure 10.6   Structure chart for Exercises 10.3.1 and 10.3.2

used for Exercise 10.2.1. The modified listing is shown below. Only the listing for the staircase function is shown. This waveform appears as a sawtooth on a CRO if it is viewed on a fast speed. The square wave, sine wave and triangular wave functions are shown as *blank stubs*.

```
/*dac2.c   Waveform Generator */
#include <string.h>              /*for the toupper() string function*/
#include <conio.h>              /*for kbhit() function*/
#include <stdio.h>              /*for printf(),getch() functions*/
#include <dos.h>               /*for outp() function*/
#include <math.h>              /*for sin() function */
int B_Address = 0x301;          /* Port B address*/
int Control = 0x303;            /* PPI control register*/
int Config = 0x90;             /* PPI configuration*/
void Staircase();               /* Define functions*/
void Squarewave();
void Sinewave();
void Triangular();
void main()
{
    char menu;
    outp(Control,Config);        /*Configure PPI*/
    while(menu != 'Q')          /*Print a menu on screen*/
    {
        clrscr();
        printf("\033[2J\n\n\t\tWAVEFORM OUTPUT FROM D TO
            A\n");
        printf("\n\tT for sTaircase");
        printf("\n\tS for Squarewave");
        printf("\n\tI for sInewave");
        printf("\n\tR for tRiangularwave");
        printf("\n\tQ for quit\n");  /*Input a character and change it to
                                    upper case Switch to the selected
                                    function*/
        switch(toupper(getch()))
```

```
        {
            case 'T' :      Staircase();
                            break;
            case 'S' :      Squarewave();
                            break;
            case 'I' :      Sinewave();
                            break;
            case 'R' :      Triangular();
                            break;
            case 'Q' :      exit(1);
        }
    }
}
void Staircase()
{
        int i ;
        clrscr();
        printf("Hit any key for return to MENU");
        while (!kbhit())
        {
            for(i = 0; i < 256; i++)
            outp(B_Address,i);
        }
}
void Squarewave()
{       /*Blank stub*/
}
void Sinewave()
{       /*Blank Stub*/
}
void Triangular()
{       /*Blank Stub*/
}
```

Listing 10.3 .1   dac2.c

Testing Exercise 10.3.1

(i) The listing for this exercise will produce a staircase waveform, with 256 steps, on a CRO connected to the output of the DAC. Unlike the R-2R network output given in Figure 10.2, this output will increase from 0 to a positive value.

(ii) Check the linearity of the system. All the steps should be equal.

10.3.2   Exercise – complete the waveform generator

Complete the blank stubs of Listing 10.3.1. Listing 10.3.2 shows one way of producing a sine wave function. For this program to compile and run successfully the **#include < math.h >** and **#define pi 3.14** lines must be added to the beginning of Listing 10.3.1. When this program is executed and the output observed on a CRO there may be a short blank between each sine wave. This is caused by the computer taking time to reinitialise the loop.

Sinewave( ) structure
   Calculate sine amplitudes for one cycle
   Store the amplitudes in an array
   while (NOT keyboard hit)
           output the sequence of numbers from the array.

```
#include < math.h >        /*required for sin function*/
#define pi 3.14
void Sinewave()
{
   double sine[256];        /*Define an array of 255 floating point
                                           numbers*/
   int i;
   printf("\n Hit any key to return to MENU");
   for(i = 0; i < 256; i++)
              sine[i] = 128*(1 + sin(2*pi*i/256));
                             /*load sine values into arrray*/
   while (!kbhit())
   {
      for(i = 0; i < 256; i++)
          outp(B_Address,sine[i]);
   }
}
```

Listing 10.3.2

10.4   Questions   1   With reference to Figure 10.1. If Vs = 5 V, R = 5 kΩ and maximum Vo = 10 volts for a 1111 binary input. Determine:

   A.   The value of Rf.
   B.   Vo for 0001 binary input.
   C.   Vo for 1000 binary input.
2   Repeat question 10.4.1 parts B and C for a +/−5 volt output.
3   Repeat question 10.4.1 for an 8-bit DAC.

11 Analogue to digital parallel interfacing

11.1 Analogue to digital converters

11.2 A to D exercises

11.3 Questions

This chapter describes A to D conversion via the PPI port, introduced in Chapter 9.

11.1 Analogue to digital converters

The object of an analogue to digital converter (ADC) is to assign binary numbers to discrete voltage levels of an analogue signal. In an electronic system the length[1] of binary numbers must be specified. The *number length* will be, for example, 4 bits, 8 bits, 12 bits or 16 bits. Most commercial converters use 8 or 12 bits. If 8 bits are used the maximum number of levels, known as *quantising levels*, which can be assigned to a number is $2^8 = 256$. If a 2 volt maximum input is assumed, the quantising interval[2] will be $2/255 = 7.843 \, \text{mV}$. When the analogue signal does not fall exactly on a quantising level there will be a *quantising error*.

There are a large number of ADC ICs on the market which carry out conversion in several different ways. Generally, the faster the converter works, the more expensive the IC. The exercises in this chapter will only cover the conversion of very low frequencies or DC signals. With many ADCs, when AC signals are converted, some form of *sample-and-hold* circuit is required. This circuit, usually comprising a small capacitor with suitable switching, stores the instantaneous analogue voltage, while conversion of the sample to a binary number is performed. Two methods of conversion will be described in the following sections.

11.1.1 The counter ramp A to D converter

A system diagram of a 4-bit counter ramp converter is shown in Figure 11.1.

The circuit in Figure 11.1 operates as follows:

(i) An analogue signal is applied to the analogue input.

---

[1] The length of a number or code word is the number of bits.
[2] Number of intervals = number of levels −1.

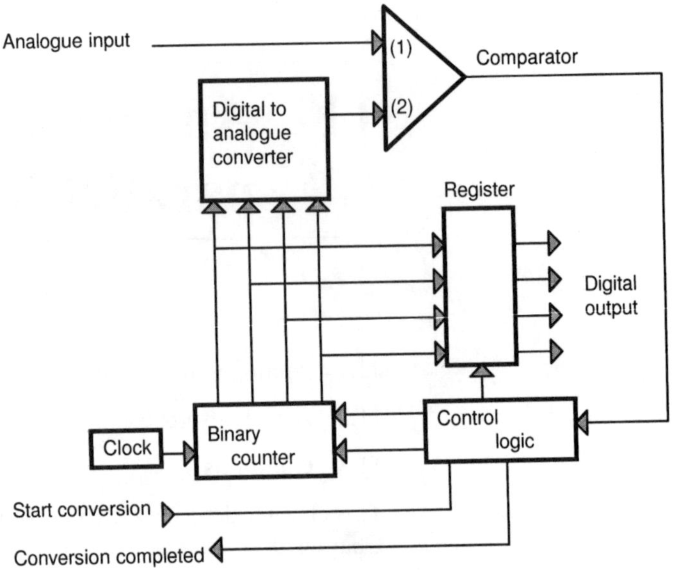

Figure 11.1   Counter ramp ADC

(ii) The **start conversion** line is asserted (counter reset).

(iii) The counter counts up from zero.

(iv) The DAC converts the counter output to an analogue signal.

(v) The comparator compares the output from the DAC with the analogue input. When (2) > (1) the comparator output stops the counter via the control logic.

(vi) The control logic enables the output register and hence loads the counter output into the register.

(vii) The **conversion completed** line is asserted.

The major disadvantage of the counter ramp ADC is its relatively long conversion time for large input signals, this arises from the fact that the DAC must ramp up from zero. The maximum conversion speed is limited by the time taken for the DAC output to settle after each counter increment.

The conversion time of the counter ramp is proportional to the clock frequency, and the number of quantising levels into which the analogue signal is divided. An 8-bit ADC has 256 quantising levels. Conversion time must be allowed for the maximum input. Hence the conversion will take 256 clock pulses. If a 1 MHz clock is used, the period of each clock pulse is 1 µs. The conversion time will therefore be 256 µs.

Figure 11.2 shows a timing diagram for a 4-bit counter ramp ADC. In this diagram the analogue input produces a binary output of 1001 = 9.

11.1.2   Flash A to D converter

Using a bank of comparators is an alternative and much faster way of converting analogue signals to binary codes. This method is rather

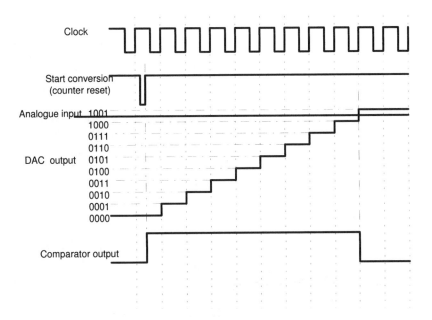

Figure 11.2 4-bit counter ramp timing diagram

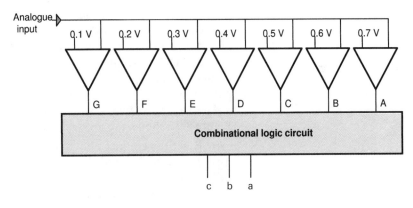

3-bit digital output

Figure 11.3 3-bit flash ADC

Inputs							Outputs		
A	**B**	**C**	**D**	**E**	**F**	**G**	**a**	**b**	**c**
0	0	0	0	0	0	0	0	0	0
0	0	0	0	0	0	1	0	0	1
0	0	0	0	0	1	1	0	1	0
0	0	0	0	1	1	1	0	1	1
0	0	0	1	1	1	1	1	0	0
0	0	1	1	1	1	1	1	0	1
0	1	1	1	1	1	1	1	1	0
1	1	1	1	1	1	1	1	1	1

Figure 11.4 Truth table for flash ADC logic circuit

expensive as it requires a comparator for each quantising level. Figure 11.3 is a logic diagram of a 3-bit flash converter. All the comparator outputs which have reference voltages below the input level will change estate. A combinational logic circuit then converts the comparator outputs to 3-bit binary codes. Figure 11.4 is a truth table of the logic circuit.

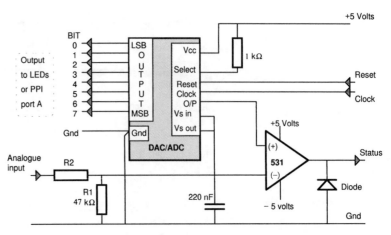

Figure 11.5   Counter ramp ADC circuit

11.2   A to C exercises

The exercises in this chapter use the ZN 425E as an ADC.

11.2.1   Exercise – ADC test

The aim of this exercise is to construct an ADC board using a counter ramp IC which works via the PPI. Both the software listing and the hardware circuit are provided.

If the clock signal is produced by the software, it is possible to design a system which only needs three control connections to the computer (*reset* and *clock*, and the *status*). The binary output equals the number of clock pulses supplied by the computer.

If an ADC is used in which the digital output is not proportional to the number of clock pulses, the output will need to be read into the computer parallel port.

The hardware and software may be developed and tested separately. Figure 11.5 shows the logic circuit which operates as follows:

(i)   Reset the counter and start the clock.
(ii)   The ADC is ramped up one step with each **clock** pulse.
(iii)   When the ADC O/P rises above the applied **analogue input** the output of the **comparator** changes state.
(iv)   The **conversion status** signal is used to stop the clock.
(v)   The ADC binary output is read.

The components used in Figure 11.5 are listed below:

Quantity	Item	Comments
1	ZN425 ADC	As used in Chapter 10
1	531 comparator	The pin assignment is the same as a 741 op. amp. A 741 may be substituted for the 531
2	47 kΩ resistors	R2, which is used to set the dynamic range, has a starting value of 47 kΩ
1	1 kΩ resistor	
1	220 nF capacitor	
1	Small silicon diode	This prevents the output from going below 0 volts

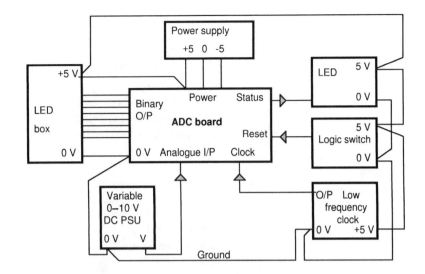

Figure 11.6   Test circuit connections

Testing the circuit

The test connections are shown in Figure 11.6 and are listed below:

(i) *LED box* to the **binary output** of the ADC.

(ii) A variable *DC 0 to 10 volt source* to the **analogue input**.

(iii) A *logic switch* to the **reset input**.

(iv) An *LED* or *voltmeter* to the **status output**.

(v) A *manual or low frequency clock* pulse generator to the **clock input**.

Operation:

(vi) Set the *variable input voltage* to **10 volts**.

(vii) *Switch reset* to **logic 0** and then to **logic 1**. The *status output* should go **high** (logic 1).

(viii) Start the clock. The *LEDs* on the LED box should **count up from 0**.

(ix) When the *status* goes **low** (logic 0). *Stop* the **clock**.

(x) *Repeat from (vii)*, adjusting **R2** until the counter counts up to **250** when **10 volts** is applied.

(xi) Check for correct counting when lower voltages are applied.

Software structure for Exercise 11.2.1

Define RESET = 0, MARK = 3, SPACE = 1, STATE *input status*
Initialise PPI
Print instructions
while(NO keyboard input)
{
   RESET
   Wait for Logic 0 on STATUS
   do

```
        {
          MARK
          Increment count
          Test for Maximum Count
          SPACE
          Short delay
        }while(STATE equals 0)
        print Reading on Binary Input
    }
}
```

```
/* adctest.c ADC test Connected to PPI board */
#include <conio.h>                /*for kbhit() function*/
#include <stdio.h>               /*for printf(),getch() functions*/
#include <dos.h>                 /*for outp() function*/
                                 /*RESET CLOCK*/
#define RESET outp(0x302,0)      /*C0 to 0 C1 to 0*/
#define MARK outp(0x302,3)       /*C0 to 1 C1 to 1*/
#define SPACE outp(0x302,1)      /*C0 to 1 C1 to 0*/
#define STATE (inp(0x302) & 16)  /*Inputs the status on C4 and
                                   mask for bit 4 only*/
int A_Address = 0x300;           /*Address of PPI Port A */
int Control = 0x303;             /*Address of PPI control
                                   register*/

int Config = 0x9A;              /*A = In, B = In, CL = Out,
                                   CH = In*/

void main()
{
    int count;
    outp(Control,Config);
    clrscr();
    printf("\n\n ADC Test");
    printf("\n\n Press any Key to Quit");
    while(!kbhit())
    {
        RESET;
        count = 0;
        printf("\033[14;10H Waiting for Logic 0 on STATUS");
        do
        {
            if(kbhit())
                    exit(1);
        }while(STATE != 0);
        printf("\033[14;10H Status = 0 Sending Clock ");
        do
        {
            MARK;
```

```
                    if (++count > 255)
                        printf("\033[16;10H Maximum Input Exceeded ");
                    else
                    {
                        SPACE;
                        delay(50);
                        printf("*");        /*For testing the program*/
                    }
                }while(STATE == 0);
                printf("\033[16;10H Reading = %d     ",inp(A_Address));
        }
}
```

Listing 11.2.1   adctest.c

Testing 11.2.1 software

  (i) Connect a *logic switch* to the **status** (input) **C4**.
 (ii) Connect an *LED* to the **reset** (output) **C0**.
(iii) Connect an *LED* to the **clock** (Outputs) **C1**.
 (iv) Switch *status* to **logic 1**.
  (v) Run the program. *Reset* and *clock* LEDs should be **OFF**. The screen should show 'Waiting for *logic 0* on **status**'.
 (vi) Switch *status* to **logic 0**.
(vii) The *reset* LED should go to **ON**.
(viii) The *clock* LED should repeatedly switch **ON OFF**. The screen should show 'Status logic 0. Sending clock'.
 (ix) Switch **status** to **logic 1**. The operations from (vi) are repeated.
  (x) The screen should show the number read in from a *switch* box connected to **port A**.

Testing the system

  (i) Make the following connections between the ADC board and PPI ports:

        Reset   to   C0
        Clock   to   C1
        Status   to   C4
        Binary output   to   Port A

 (ii) With the *variable DC voltage* connected to the **analogue input**, run the program.
(iii) Varying the *DC input from 0 to 10 volts* should proportionally change the count. Write down a table, noting the number displayed for half volt steps. Draw a graph of the *output numbers* against the **input voltages**.

11.2.2   Exercise – voltmeter

In this exercise the hardware used for Exercise 11.2.1 is incorporated into a voltmeter interface. The voltmeter is to read voltages up to 10 volts and must have a high input impedance ($>1\,\mathrm{M\Omega}$). Listing 11.2.1 needs a little modification so that '**Overload**' is displayed on the screen when the count exceeds 250.

One way to achieve a *high input impedance* is to use a simple op. amp. buffer circuit as shown in Figure 11.7. With this circuit the input op. amp. must have a DC supply of $+/-12$ volts. The only other modification to the hardware is to adjust R2 so that 10 V is represented by a count of 250.

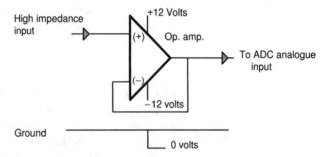

Figure 11.7   High impedance input circuit

11.2.3   Exercise – two-range voltmeter

This exercise may be considered as a project. The aim is to add a 0-to-1 volt range to the meter. The range selection should be automatic or from the computer keyboard. Note an additional control line is required. Figure 11.8 shows the system diagram, and Figure 11.9 shows one way of changing the gain of the op. amp. input circuit.

An analogue switch or relay may be used to change gain resistors in order to obtain two ranges. The voltage gain of Figure 11.9 is given by the equation:

$$G_V = \frac{10 + R}{10} \quad \text{where R is the value of one of the resistors in k}\Omega$$

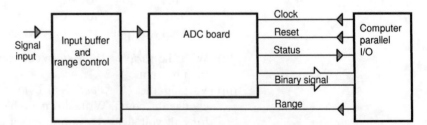

Figure 11.8   System diagram of two-range voltmeter

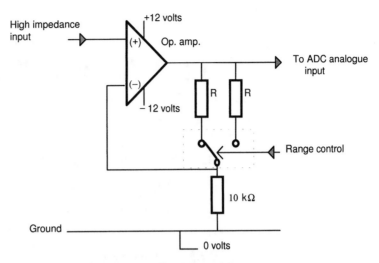

Figure 11.9   High impedance input circuit

11.3 Questions An 8-bit counter ramp ADC has a clock frequency of 2 MHz and a maximum input of 0 to 5 volts. Determine:

1 The conversion time for a 5 volt signal.
2 The conversion time for a 1 volt signal.
3 If 1 volt is not on an exact quantising level, the binary code representing it will cause a quantising error. Express this error as a percentage of 1 volt.

12 The parallel printer port

12.1 The parallel printer port

12.2 Output/Input exercises

12.3 Stepper motor exercises

12.4 Waveform generator exercises

12.5 Voltmeter exercises

The exercises described in previous chapters are repeated in this chapter using the parallel printer port.

12.1 The parallel printer port

The advantages of using the printer port are:

 (i) No additional cards are needed for the computer.
(ii) The pin numbers are standard for all PCs.

The disadvantages are:

 (i) The printer must be disconnected when doing experiments.
(ii) It is less flexible and there are fewer bits available.

The parallel printer port is a 25-way, D-type, female socket. There are three addresses associated with this port (**base**, **base + 1**, **base + 2**). The actual **base** address may be found from information supplied with the computer or by running System Check software.

Typical base addresses are **378 hex** or **3BC hex**.

This port has eight data output bits and a number of control bits. Some of the control bits are outputs, some inputs, and some can be programmed for either inputs or outputs. The logic levels are TTL (0 and 5 volts) like the PPI. The most convenient outputs and inputs have been selected for exercises in this book, although a few more are available. The outputs, at the **base** address, are on pins 2 to 8 with the least significant bit (LSB) on pin 2. There are five input bits at address **base + 1**, these are assigned as shown in Figure 12.1.

12.2 Output/Input exercises

12.2.1 Exercise – output data via the printer port

This is a repeat of Exercise 9.1.2. The aim of this exercise is to show that the output system is working correctly by sending binary numbers to the

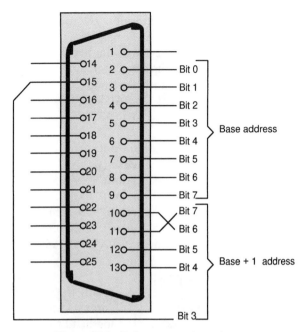

Figure 12.1 Printer port pin assignment

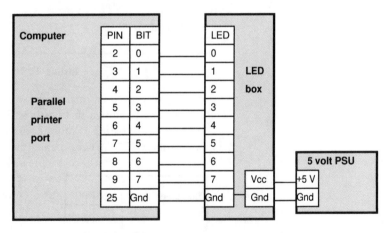

Figure 12.2 Printer port connections to LED box

base address of the Printer Port. The hardware connections are shown in Figure 12.2.

12.2.2 Exercise – input/output data via the printer port

This exercise tests for both input and output of data. Binary numbers are read from a switch box connected to **base + 1** pins of the printer port. The

```
/*outprint.c   Output data to Printer Port. Pins 2 to 9 connected to
an LED box. */
#include < dos.h >
#include < stdio.h >
#include < conio.h >
int Out_Address = 0x3bc;              /*Base address of printer port*/
void main()
{
      int data,error = 1;
      clrscr();
      printf("\033[5;5H Enter two Hexadecimal digits");
      printf("\033[7;5H Any other letter key to Quit");
      printf("\033[8;5H and press ENTER");
      printf("\033[20;5H
Address %0X",Out_Address);
      do
  {
          printf("\033[5;37H      ");
          gotoxy(35,5);
          fflush(stdin);
          error = scanf("%2X",&data);        /*Data from keyboard*/
          outp(Out_Address,data);      /*Send the data to the port*/
  }
  while(error != 0);
}
```

Listing 12.2.1   outprint.c

output is displayed as in the previous exercise. The additional hardware connections are shown in Figure 12.3.

The software listing is more complex than usual and introduces some new techniques. A structure chart is shown in Figure 12.4. Compile and

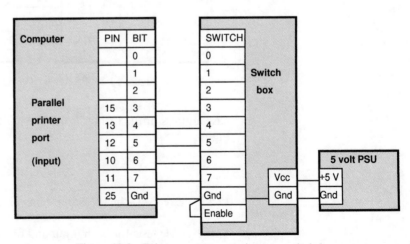

Figure 12.3   Printer port connections to switch box

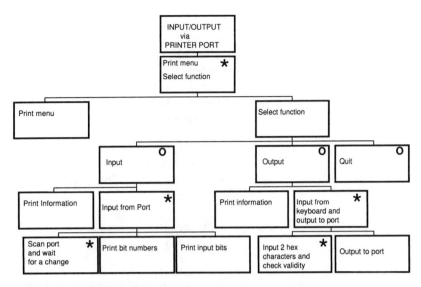

Figure 12.4 Structure chart for Exercise 12.2.2

Listing time	data	i	INPUT	k	valid	ptr	ptr-valid	<< 4*i
	0							
for (i = 1; i > -1; i++) k = toupper(getch()) ptr = strchr(valid,k) data = (ptr-valid) << 4*i data = data +	20 hex	1	'2'	'2'	FFD8	FFDA	2	20 hex
for (i = 1; i > -1; i++ k = toupper(getch()) ptr = strchr(valid,k) data = data +	2B hex	0	'b'	'B'	FFD8	FFE3	B	B hex

Note: The **valid** address will be derived during program run time.

Figure 12.5 Trace table for boxed-in section of Listing 12.2.2

run the program. The inputs from the switch box will be displayed on the screen. Note the input from bit 7 is inverted. A trace table of the boxed-in section of the listing is shown in Figure 12.5.

Referring to the trace table, Figure 12.5, for the boxed-in section of Listing 12.2.2, in order to input two hexadecimal characters without using the Enter key, **getch()** is used twice with the **for()** function. The input is checked for a valid hexadecimal number and then changed to binary. The two inputs from the keyboard are combined to form an 8-bit binary code.

```
/*inoutptr.c Input is from parallel printer port base address. Output
data to base +1 address. Port Input should be connected to a
switch box. Port Output should be connected to an LED box.*/
#include < dos.h >
#include < stdio.h >
#include < string.h >
#include < conio.h >
void Input();
void Output();
int Out_Address = 0x3bc;      /*Insert base address of printer port*/
int In_Address = 0x3bd; /*Insert base address plus one*/
void main()
{
   int menu;
   while (1)
   {
      clrscr();
      printf("\033[5;5H DATA INPUT / OUTPUT");
      printf("\033[7;5H[I]nput from Printer Port %3x", In_Address);
      printf("\033[8;5H[O]output to Printer Port %3x",Out_Address);
      printf("\033[9;5H[Q]uit");
      menu = toupper(getch());
      switch(menu)
      {
         case 'T' :  Input();
                     break;
         case 'O' :  Output();
                     break;
         case 'Q' :  exit(1);
      }
   }
}
void Input()
{
   int data,change,i;
   clrscr();
   printf("\033[5;5H Press any key for main menu ");
   printf("\033[7;5H Connections to 25 pin D type Printer Port");
   printf("\033[8;5H Pin 15 FAULT = bit 3");
   printf("\033[9;5H Pin 13 SLCT = bit 4");
   printf("\033[10;5H Pin 12 PE = bit 5");
   printf("\033[11;5H Pin 10 ACKNLG = bit 6");
   printf("\033[12;5H Pin 11 BUSY = bit 7 Inverted");
   printf("\033[20;10H Address %0X",In_Address);
   while(1)
   {
      do
      {
         change = inp(In_Address);
```

```
                    if (kbhit()) return;
                  }while (change = = data);
                  data = change;
                  printf("\033[13;5H Data input = %2x",data);
                  printf("\033[15;5H Bits 7 6 5 4 3");
                  printf("\033[16;5H State ");
                  for(i = 7;i > 2;i- -)
                      printf(" %1x",(data≫i)&1);
          }
      }
      void Output()
      {
          int i,data;
          char valid[17] = "0123456789ABCDEF";
          char k, *ptr;
          clrscr();
          printf("\033[5;5H Enter two Hexadecimal digits");
          printf("\033[7;5H Any other key for MENU ");
          printf("\033[20;5H Address %0X Hex",Out_Address);
          while(1) /*set up continuous loop*/
              {
              data = 0;
              printf("\033[10;37H");

              gotoxy(35,5);
              for (i = 1;i > -1;i--)        /*input to Hex Character*/
                  {
                      k = toupper(getche());
                      if((ptr = strchr(valid,k)) = = 0)
                              return;    /*Return to menu if input not valid*/
                      data = data + (ptr-valid) ≪ (i*4);
                  }    /* See trace table below*/

              outp(Out_Address,data);  /*Send the data to the port*/
              }
      }
```

Figure 12.2.2   inoutptr.c

12.3 Stepper motor exercises   These exercises are a repeat of the stepper motor exercises described in Chapter 9.

12.3.1   Exercise – stepper motor; two speeds in each direction

The aim of these exercises is to develop a C program to control the speed and direction of a stepper motor. The motor and four switches from a switch box are connected to the printer port, see Figure 12.6. The software structure is shown in Figure 9.14.

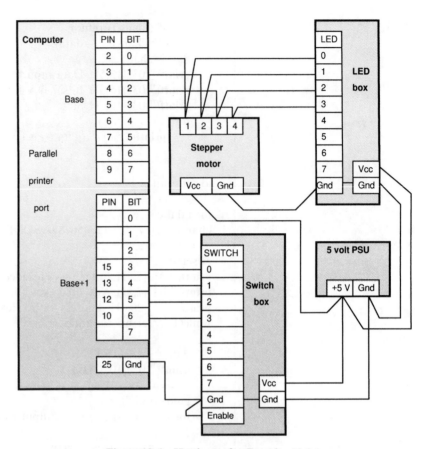

Figure 12.6   Hardware for Exercise 12.3.1

The delays in the program must be adjusted so that the motor runs fast and slow smoothly. The first delay for each sequence is made shorter to allow for computer time when looping back. If the motor code is sent too quickly, the motor will vibrate.

```
/*motorptr.c motor control. Speed and direction of motor
controlled from Printer Port.
Pins 15, 13, 12 and 10 should be connected to a switch box.
Pins 2, 3, 4 and 5 should be connected to an LED box and motor.*/
#include < dos.h >
#include < stdio.h >
#include < string.h >
#include < conio.h >
int Out_Address = 0x3bc;        /*Base  address  of  printer  port*/
int In_Address = 0x3bd;         /*Base+ 1 address of printer port*/
int clockwise = 0;
int anticlockwise = 1;
int slow = 100;    /*These two speeds are adjusted according to the
                                                speed of the */
```

```
in fast = 10;        /* computer. The higher the number the slower the
                                                        motor*/
void Rotate(int,int);
void main()
{
   int K = 1;
   clrscr();
   printf("\033[5;5H STEPPER MOTOR CONTROL");
   printf("\033[6;5H Control the motor from the switch box");
   printf("\033[7;5H If all switches are at logic 0");
   printf("the motor will stop");
   printf("\033[9;5H HIT ANY KEY TO QUIT PROGRAM");
   printf("\033[11;5H BIT NUMBER MODE");
   printf("\033[12;5H 0  1 slow clockwise");
   printf("\033[13;5H 1  2 fast clockwise");
   printf("\033[14;5H 2  4 fast anticlockwise");
   printf("\033[15;5H 3  8 slow anticlockwise");
   printf("\033[17;5H Number input = ");
   do
   {
           /*Input and shift 3 bits to the right*/
        K = ((inp(In_Address)≫3) & 0x0F);
        printf("\033[17;22H %li ",K);
        switch(K)
        {
            case 1   : Rotate(slow,clockwise);
                       break;
            case 2   : Rotate(fast,clockwise);
                       break;
            case 4   : Rotate(fast,anticlockwise);
                       break;
            case 8   : Rotate(slow,anticlockwise);
                       break;
            default  : printf("\033[20;10H Motor stopped");
        }
   } while(!kbhit());
   clrscr();
}
void Rotate(int speed, int direction)
{
   int i;
   int data[2][4] = {3,6,12,9, /*Code for rotate clockwise*/
               9,12,6,3}; /*Code for rotate anti clockwise*/
   delay(speed*9/10);
   printf("\033[20;10H.............");
   for(i = 0;i < 4;i + +)
   {
       outp(Out_Address,data[direction][i]); /*Send code to motor*/
       delay(speed);
   }
}
```

Figure 12.3.1   motorptr.c

12.3.2   Exercise – stepper motor; three speeds in each direction

Modify the software to provide for slow, medium and fast speeds of the motor in each direction. One way of doing this is to use one switch to select direction and the other three switches to select slow, medium or fast.

12.3.3   Exercise – two motors, two speeds

Modify the original system to control two stepper motors from one set of four switches.

12.4   Waveform generator exercises

12.4.1   Exercise – waveform generator

This is a repeat of Exercise 10.3 using the printer port. The aim of this exercise is to construct a D to A interface circuit and connect it to the PC parallel printer port. The software structure and testing for this exercise are fully described in Chapter 10, so only the circuit, Figure 12.7, and software listing will be given here. In the circuit example a ZN425E DAC/ADC IC is used. As previously stated the hardware and software should be developed and tested separately.

A power supply with outputs +5, 0, −5 is required for this exercise. In addition to the components shown in the circuit of Figure 12.7, an LED box may be connected in parallel with the input block to give added information. Pin assignments for the ICs are given in Chapter 10.

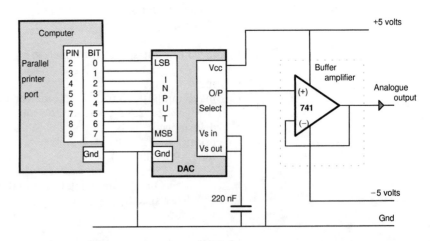

Figure 12.7   D to A logic circuit for Exercise 12.4.1

```
/*wformptr   Waveform Generator */

#include < string.h >          /*for the toupper() string function*/
#include < conio.h >           /*for kbhit() function*/
#include < stdio.h >           /*for printf(),getch() functions*/
#include < dos.h >             /*for outp() function*/
#include < math.h >            /*for sin() function */
int Out_Address = 0x3bc;       /* Printer Port Base Address*/
void Staircase();              /* Define functions*/
void Squarewave();
void Sinewave();
void Triangular();
void main()
{
   while(1)                    /*Print a menu on screen*/
   {
       clrscr();
       printf("\033[2J\n\n\t\tWAVEFORM OUTPUT FROM D TO
              A\n");
       printf("\n\tT for sTaircase");
       printf("\n\tS for Squarewave");
       printf("\n\tI for sInewave");
       printf("\n\tR for tRiangularwave");
       printf("\n\tQ for quit\n");
       switch(toupper(getch()))
       {
               case 'T' :      Staircase();
                               break;
               case 'S' :      Squarewave();
                               break;
               case 'I' :      Sinewave();
                               break;
               case 'R' :      Triangular();
                               break;
               case 'Q' :      exit(1);
       }
   }
}
void Staircase()
{
   int i ;
   clrscr();
   printf("Hit any key for return to MENU");
   while (!kbhit())
   {
       for(i = 0; i < 256; i++)
       {
               outp(Out_Address,i);
```

Listing 12.4.1   wformptr.c

```
                        delay(50); /*for test purposes only*/
            }
        }
    }
    void Squarewave()
    { /*Blank stub*/
    }
    void Sinewave()
    { /*Blank Stub*/
    }
    void Triangular()
    { /*Blank Stub*/
    }
```

Listing 12.4.1 (*cont.*)

12.4.2 Exercise – complete the waveform generator

Complete the blank stubs of Listing 12.4.1. Listing 10.3.2 shows one way of producing a sine wave function. For this program to compile and run successfully #**define pi 3.14** must be added to the beginning of Listing 12.4.1. When this program is executed and the output observed on a CRO there may be a short blank between each sine wave. This is caused by the computer taking time to reinitialise the loop.

12.5 Voltmeter exercises

12.5.1 Exercise – ADC

The voltmeter exercise has been previously described in Chapter 11 with input via the PPI. These exercises can only be done via the printer port if the ADC output is proportional to the number of clock pulses supplied, like the counter ramp described in Chapter 11. The aim of this exercise is to construct an ADC board, using a counter ramp IC. Only three signal connections between the board and computer are required, **clock**, **reset** and **status**. The binary number representing the analogue input is equal to the number of clock pulses counted and supplied by the computer. The circuit diagram is shown in Figure 12.8, the structure chart in Figure 12.9, and program in Listing 12.5.1, the components are the same as the ADC board described in Chapter 11.

The circuit should be tested as described below, and then connected to the computer.

The circuit of Figure 12.8 operates as follows:

(i) Following *reset* the output of the ZN425 is ramped up one step with each clock pulse.

(ii) When the O/P of the ADC goes above the applied *analogue input* the **comparator output** will change state.

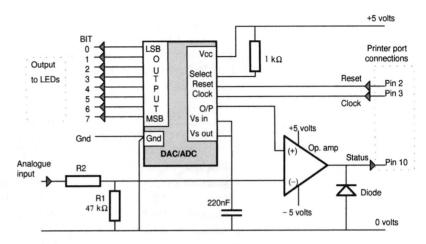

Figure 12.8   Counter ramp ADC circuit

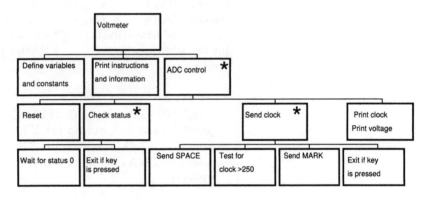

Figure 12.9   Structure chart for Exercise 12.5.1

(iii) The *conversion status signal* changes state and causes the computer to stop sending **clock pulses**.

(iv) The ADC binary *output* equals the number of **clock pulses** supplied.

Testing the circuit
Make the following connections:

   (i) *LED* box to the **binary output** of the ADC.
  (ii) A variable *DC 0 to 10 volt source* to the **analogue input**.
 (iii) A *logic switch* to the **reset** input.
  (iv) An *LED* to the **status** output.
   (v) A *manual* or *low frequency clock generator* to the **clock input**.

Operation:

  (vi) Set the *variable input voltage* to **10 volts**.
 (vii) Switch *reset* to **logic 0** and then to **logic 1**.
(viii) Start the **clock**.

(ix) The *status output* should go **high**.

(x) The *LEDs* on the LED box should count up from 0.

(xi) When the *status* goes **low**, stop the clock.

(xii) Repeat from (vii), adjusting **R2** until the counter counts up to 250.

(xiii) Check for correct counting when other voltages are applied.

```c
/*adc2ptr.c   Voltmeter basic program */
/*Connected to Printer Port, Reset pin 2, Clock pin3, Reset pin 10*/
#include <string.h>          /*for the toupper() string function*/
#include <conio.h>           /*for kbhit() function*/
#include <stdio.h>           /*for printf(),getch() functions*/
#include <dos.h>             /*for outp() function*/
#define STATUS       (inp(In_Address) & 64)
                             /*Brackets required because of spaces i*/
#define RESET         outp(Out_Address,0)
#define SPACE         outp(Out_Address,1)
#define MARK          outp(Out_Address,3)
int Out_Address = 0x3bc;    /* Printer port output address*/
int In_Address = 0x3bd;     /* Printer port input address*/
void main()
{
    int clock;
    printf("\033[2J\n\n\t ADC TEST\n");
    printf("\n\tRESET out on pin 2");
    printf("\n\tCLOCK out on pin 3");
    printf("\n\tSTATUS in on pin 10");
    while(1)
    {
        clock = 0;
        RESET;
        printf("\033[10;10H Waiting for STATUS to go LOW ");
        do
        {
            if (kbhit())
                exit(1);
        }while(STATUS != 0);
        printf("\033[10;10H Sending clock pulses until STATUS goes
            HIGH ");
        do
        {
            SPACE;
            printf("\033[14;10H        ");
            if (clock++ >250)
            {
                printf("\033[16;10H O V E R L O A D\n");
                clock = 0;
            }
```

```
            MARK ;
            printf("\033[14;10H %i",clock);        /*Program test only*/
            if (kbhit())
                exit(1);
        }while(STATUS == 0);
        printf("\033[16;10H  Data = %i            ",clock);
    }
}
```

Listing 12.5.1   adc2ptr.c

12.5.2   Exercise – voltmeter

In this exercise the hardware used for Exercise 12.5.1 is incorporated into a voltmeter interface. The voltmeter is to read voltages up to 10 volts and must have a high input impedance ($>1\,\mathrm{M\Omega}$). A voltage should be output to the screen instead of the clock count.

One way to achieve the *high input impedance* is to use an op. amp. buffer circuit, as shown in Figure 12.10. With this circuit the input op. amp. must have a DC supply of $+/-12$ volts.

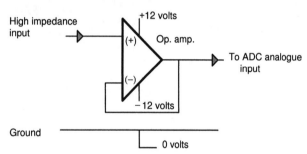

Figure 12.10   High impedance input circuit

12.5.3   Exercise – two-range voltmeter

This exercise may be considered as a project. The aim is to add a 0-to-1 volt range to the meter. The range selection should be automatic or from the computer keyboard. Note an additional control line is required. Figure 12.11 shows the system diagram.

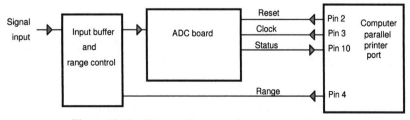

Figure 12.11   System diagram of two-range voltmeter

The input buffer and range control, which must have a high input impedance, may be an op. amp. An analogue switch, or a relay, may be used to change gain resistors in order to obtain two ranges, see Chapter 11.

13 Additional exercises

13.1 Frequency counter theory

13.2 Frequency counter exercises

13.3 Serial data communication

13.4 Stepper motor control via serial link

This chapter describes two exercises which may be developed into interesting projects. Preceding each exercise is a brief theoretical introduction.

13.1 Frequency counter theory

A frequency counter is an electronic circuit which counts the number of cycles produced by an alternating source in a given period.

The basic interface, Figure 13.1, consists of a *Schmitt trigger* to square up the input signal; a *logic* gate to pass the signal for a given period; and a *binary counter* to count the cycles. The Schmitt trigger and the gate are combined in one IC. These devices are described below.

The count commences with a *reset* signal, which resets the counter to zero. The gate *input* control signal then opens the gate. This allows rectangular pulses from the Schmitt trigger to be applied to the clock input of the counter. The counting period is determined by the software. After the signal has been given time to *settle*[1] the counter output is **read**.

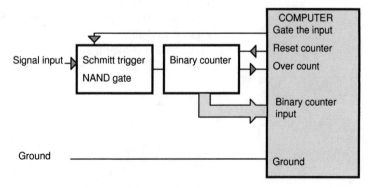

Figure 13.1 System diagram of counter

[1] The count must have time to *ripple through* the counter.

The period of the *gated input* must be made variable so that the system can be calibrated to display the correct frequency.

13.1.1   The Schmitt trigger

A Schmitt trigger circuit is effectively an interface between an *analogue* input and a *digital* circuit. It effectively squares up the input signal so that the rise and fall times[2] are suitable for application to a logic circuit. Analogue signals may have an infinite number of voltage or current levels between a minimum and maximum value, whereas digital signals have two[3] discrete levels. Signals which do not have fast rise and fall times are unsuitable as inputs to logic circuits for the following reasons:

 (i) TTL devices tend to become unstable when the output changes state, causing a *grassy effect* after the change.
(ii) CMOS devices tend to overheat due to both logic 0 and logic 1 FETs being switched on at the same time.

The basic feature of a Schmitt trigger circuit is that its *transfer characteristic* contains a **hysteresis loop**, as shown in Figure 13.3. In the characteristic shown, the input signal must rise to 1.6 volts before the output changes from logic 1 to logic 0. The input must fall to 0.8 volts before the output changes back to logic 1. Hence if the input changes slowly there is no instability caused by switching on a single threshold. A typical IC is the 74xx13 which has two 4 input NAND gates incorporating Schmitt trigger circuits.

   With a NAND gate, if all four inputs are at logic 1 the output is logic 0, for all other input combinations the output is at logic 1. Figure 13.4 is a typical standard NAND gate transfer characteristic for comparison.

13.1.2   The binary counter

Binary counters are built up from bistable gates or transistor circuits. Bistables, also known as flip-flops (FF) have two stable output states, logic 0 and logic 1. The output state of a bistable may be changed by one of the following four input changes, depending on circuit design.

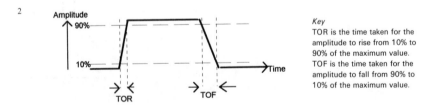

2

Amplitude

Key
TOR is the time taken for the amplitude to rise from 10% to 90% of the maximum value.
TOF is the time taken for the amplitude to fall from 90% to 10% of the maximum value.

[3] In some communication systems digital signals have a number of discrete levels.

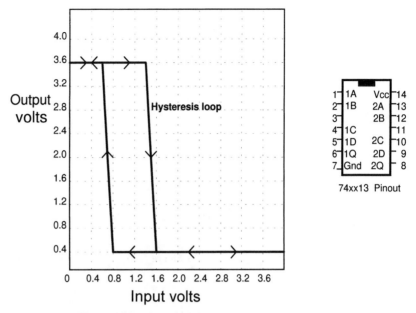

Figure 13.3 A typical Schmitt trigger characteristic

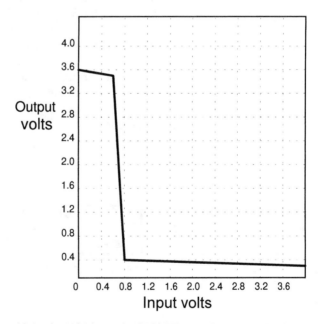

Figure 13.4 A typical standard NAND gate input/output characteristic

(i) Change of state from 0 to 1.
(ii) Change of state from 1 to 0.
(iii) A negative-going edge.
(iv) A positive-going edge.

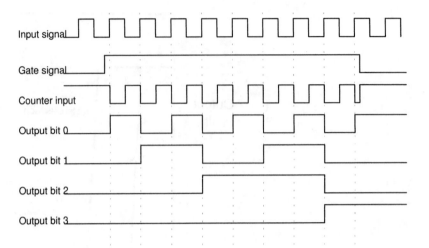

Figure 13.5   Binary ripple-through counter, timing diagram

Figure 13.5 illustrates how a binary counter counts nine cycles of the input signal. At the end of the gate period, bit $0 = $ logic 1, bits 1 and $2 = $ logic 0 and bit $3 = $ logic 1. Hence binary $1001 = 9_{10}$. The frequency measured depends on the period of the gating signal.

Although there are several variations of binary counter design, in this exercise only circuits known as ripple-through counters will be used. A ripple-through counter is a circuit where the output of one bistable is directly connected to the input of the next bistable as shown in Figure 13.6. The output frequency of a bistable equals half the input frequency.

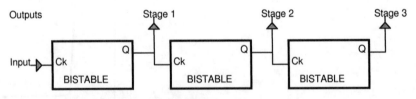

Figure 13.6   A three-stage ripple-through binary counter

The CMOS 4020 is a suitable IC for the following exercises. This is a 14-stage binary ripple-through counter, with clock and reset inputs. The output from each stage changes state on the negative-going edge of the input signal to that stage.

The logic diagram is shown in Figure 13.7. The denary value of each bit is equal to 2^N. Where N is the stage number. Note that the outputs from stages 2 and 3 are not available.

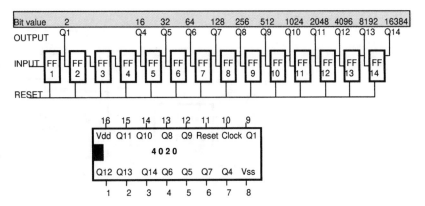

Figure 13.7 Logic diagram and pin assignment of a 4020 counter

13.2 Frequency counter exercises

The following exercises use the 4020 for measuring frequency.

13.2.1 Exercise – basic counter

The aim of this exercise is to develop a frequency counter interface board and associated software for a personal computer using the PPI port. The counter will measure and display frequencies on the monitor screen. The input signal amplitude should be between 2 and 5 volts. See the logic circuit Figure 13.8.

The logic circuit may be constructed either on proto-board or on strip-board.

It is always advisable to check the operation of the hardware before connecting it to the computer. Figure 13.9 shows the test set-up. The signal generator is adjusted to output a suitable frequency. Two logic switches are used to operate the gate and reset inputs. The LEDs will show if the counter is working. The over-count indicator should also be checked using an LED. To ensure satisfactory operation of the Schmitt trigger, the signal to be measured should have a **minimum pk-to-pk value of 0 to +2 volts** and a **maximum pk-to-pk value of 0 to 5 volts**.

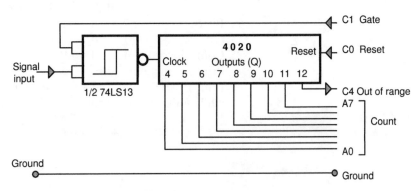

Figure 13.8 Frequency counter logic circuit

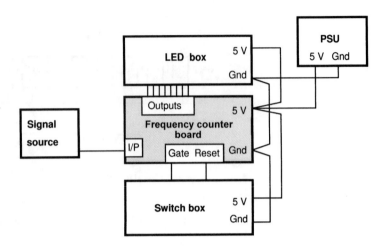

Figure 13.9 Frequency counter test set-up

Referring to the logic circuit, Figure 13.8, when a logic 1 is received on A0 through to A7, the number of cycles counted will be equal to the sum of 2^4 to 2^{11}. Hence maximum count equals:

$$16 + 32 + 64 + 128 + 256 + 512 + 1024 + 2048 = 4080$$

The count increases by 1 for every 16 cycles of input. To obtain the correct number of input cycles, the software multiplies the count by 16 and then adds 8 which gives an accuracy of ± 8 cycles. The frequency measured will depend upon the time for which the input gate is open. It is necessary to give a short period of a few milliseconds after the gate is closed before reading the counter. This ensures that all the changes have rippled through.

Software structure for Exercise 13.2.1
Initialise PPI,
        PORT A is used to input the count
        PORT C bit 1 is used to clear the counter
        PORT C bit 0 is used to gate the input
        PORT C bit 4 receives out-of-range

Bit No.	7	6	5	4	3	2	1	0
	1	0	0	A	C_H	0	B	C_L
Control word	1	0	0	1	1	0	1	0 = 9a hex

Print instructions
Print FREQUENCY at fixed position on screen
while no keyboard input
{
        Reset counter and close gate
        Wait 1 msec
        Open input gate
        Wait for t msec
        Close input gate

Check for out-of-range
Read counter = n
Calculate cycles = ((n * 16) + 8)
Calculate frequency = cycles*1000/t
Print count and frequency
Clear counter {C0 to logic 0}

}
exit

13.2.2   Exercise – four-range counter

The frequency range measured by the interface may be changed by changing the count period and multiplying the input from port A accordingly. Modify the software to provide four ranges which can be selected from a **menu**. The menu should also include an *auto* position so that the range is selected automatically. The automatic selection will work faster if the counter tries the highest range first, and then moves down to the next range if the count is below a given value. Alternatively the counter could try the lowest frequency range first and then try the next if the **out-of-range** signal is detected.

Possible counter ranges

Range	Frequency band (Hz)	Accuracy (±Hz)
1	8 to 4088	8
2	32 to 16352	32
3	64 to 32704	64
4	128 to 65408	128

Figure 13.10   Frequency counter ranges

13.2.3   Exercise – improve the accuracy to ±1 Hz

Use a 4-bit counter, such as a 74LS93, to obtain the stages which are not available on the 4020. Both ports A and B are used to input a 14-bit number, giving a possible count of 0-to-32767. If port A is used for the lower 8 bits and port B for the upper 6 bits, the count calculation is:

$$count = inp(A\_Address) + (inp(B\_Address)\ \&\ 0x3F) * 512$$

Note the 3F hex masks out the two unused bits on port B.

```
/*counter.c   This program sends a counter clear signal from C1, a gate signal from
C0, and inputs the counter reading on port A. The gate delay will require adjustment,
depending on the speed of the computer.*/
#include < dos.h >
#include < stdio.h >
#include < math.h >
#include < conio.h >
#define RESET 2              /*(C0 Gate to logic 0, C1 Counter reset logic 1*/
#define OPEN 1               /*(C0 Gate to logic 1, C1 Counter reset logic 0*/
#define CLOSE 0              /*(C0 Gate to logic 0, C1 Counter reset logic 0*/
#define OVER 16              /*Used to check if C4 is at logic 1*/
int Count(void);
int A_Address = 0x300;       /*Insert address*/
int C_Address = 0x302;       /*Insert address*/
int Control = 0x303;         /*Insert address*/
int Config = 0x9A;           /*Insert configuration Port A to input, Port B to input,
                               Port CL to output Port CH to input */

void main()
{
   outp(Control,Config);
   outp(C_Address,0);
   clrscr();
   printf("\033[3;5H FREQUENCY COUNTER    Hit any key to Quit");
   while(!Count());
   exit(1);
}
int Count()
{
   int t = 100;              /*Change t to change frequency range*/
   float frequ,n;
   printf("\033[5;5H          ");
   outp(C_Address,RESET);
   delay(1);                 /*wait 1 msec*/
   outp(C_Address,OPEN);
   delay(t);                 /*wait t msec*/
   outp(C_Address,CLOSE);
   if (inp(C_Address) && OVER)
      printf("\033[16;10H Count out of Range          ");
   else
   {
      n = inp(A_Address);
      freq. = ((n*16) + 8)*(1000/t);
      printf("\033[16;10H COUNT %4.0f FREQUENCY %8.2f +/-8Hz",n,frequ);
   }
   return kbhit();
}
```

Listing 13.2.1   counter.c

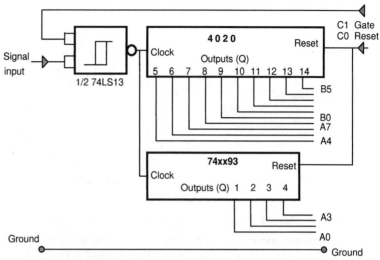

Figure 13.11   Frequency counter logic circuit

13.2.4   Exercise – auto calibration

Further develop the software so that the computer adjusts the delay time when calibrate is selected and a known frequency is applied. The software should not need calibration every time it is used. The calibration will mainly be necessary when it is installed. The delay time will therefore need to be stored in a file, so that it can be read by the program when it runs, probably while the *menu* is displayed. A possible new time would then be stored when the counter is calibrated.

13.2.5   Exercise – counter input circuit

Develop the input circuit, so that the interface board can handle a larger range of input voltage amplitudes (0.1 volt to 10 volts), and has an input impedance comparable with a typical cathode ray oscilloscope (CRO) (1 MΩ shunted by 30 pF). This exercise requires an understanding of analogue electronics. The specification of the input circuit is as follows:

(i)   High impedance input equivalent to a 1 MΩ resistor shunted by a 30 pF capacitor.
(ii) An amplifier with a gain of 20.
(iii) A clipper circuit which limits the final amplitude to a maximum of 5 volts.

The op. amp. circuit in Figure 13.12 provides a starting point. It has, however, two disadvantages:

(i)   It requires a ±5 volt supply.
(ii) The high frequency cut-off point, which depends on the type of op. amp. selected, may be too low.

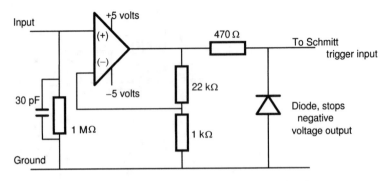

Figure 13.12   Frequency counter input circuit

13.3 Serial data communication

Chapter 8 described the computer serial output (comm. port). While this is suitable for communicating with many ancillary devices, it is limited by the fact that the output is in ASCII code. For many applications, sending data in binary code is faster and more convenient. It also allows the experimenter to structure his/her own data stream. There are several methods of sending binary data, two of which are:

(i) The data may be sent in packets with header code at the beginning. The header will include such information as the length of the packet, who it is for, and error check information.
(ii) For control purposes the code may be sent in small fixed-length bursts.

It is, of course, possible to insert a card into the computer which will send binary code. However, the only facility normally available to the experimenter is to use one or more bits of either the parallel printer port or the programmable peripheral interface (PPI) port.

The first step is to decide on the type of data to be used. If the requirement is just to send numbers then 8421BCD could be used, see Chapter 1.

Example (a)   Send 345_{10} in BCD code from bit 0 from either the printer or PPI ports.

Convert 345 into binary 001101000101_{LSB}
Place the data in a **file** and send it using the **for()** iteration:
int Out_Address = *Address of PPI Port or Printer Port*
int i;
int data[13] = {101000101100};
for (i = 0; i < 13; i++)
outp(Out_Address,i)

If any other bit of the port is used **logic 1** state is represented by 2^N. Hence if bit 3 is used, $2^3 = 8$, and the sequence in the file would be {808000808800}.

13.4 Stepper motor control via serial link

The following exercises use binary data for controlling the speed and direction of stepper motors. A 4-conductor link is used in the first exercise in order to keep the hardware as simple as possible.

13.4.1 Exercise – control of two stepper motors via a 4-conductor, serial link

The aim of this exercise is to control the speed and direction of two stepper motors via a serial link. A small serial-to-parallel interfacing circuit has to be constructed, and a C program developed. Either the PPI port or the printer port may be used.

System description
A system diagram of the interface is shown in Figure 13.13, the four conductors connected to the computer are:

clock, reset, data, ground

The shift register uses the clock, reset and data signals to convert incoming code from serial to parallel. The data register stores the code, while the next code word is being sent and converted. Each code converter changes data from 2 bits to the 4-bit format required by the motors.

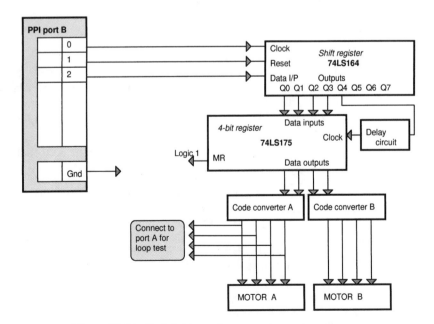

Figure 13.13 Serial driven stepper motor system diagram

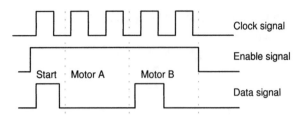

Figure 13.14 Timing diagram of a typical data signal

Stepper motor control

To control the speed and direction of a stepper motor it is necessary to provide it with a repetitive sequence of four 4-bit binary numbers. To send four different numbers only 2 bits are required, see Figure 13.15. It is also necessary to send a start bit, which will provide the shift register with an end of data word signal. Thus each data word will consist of 5 bits as shown in Figure 13.14, which illustrates the transmission of 00 to motor A and 10 to motor B.

The data signal as shown in Figure 13.14 is sent along the *data* conductor to the data **input** of the shift register. Whilst the data is being transmitted the **reset** input of the shift register is held at logic 1, via the *reset* conductor, and five clock pulses are transmitted along the *clock* conductor.

The data bits are clocked into the shift register until the start bit reaches output Q4. This output then passes through a short delay circuit and is used to strobe the shift register outputs (Q0, Q1, Q2, Q3) to the data register. Two pairs of outputs from the data register are taken to the two code-converter circuits, which generate the 4-bit code required to drive the motors.

Hardware

Code converters The code converters convert 2-bit codes into the 4-bit codes, required to drive the motors. The number sequence required to drive a motor is 3, 6, 12, 9, which arranged in binary produce the truth table Figure 13.15. Additional logic may be avoided if the inputs to the truth table are rearranged as in Figure 13.16.

From Figure 13.16 it can be seen that:

(i)   Output column **a** is the same as input column A.
(ii) Output column **b** is the same as input column B.
(iii) Output column **c** is the complement of input column A.
(iv) Output column **d** is the complement of input column B.

Hence no logic is actually required as both the true and inverted outputs are available from the data register, Figure 13.17.

The delay circuit A simple way to provide a short delay is to use two gates as shown in Figure 13.18. It will be convenient in this case to use two gates from a 74LS14. This is a hex Schmitt trigger IC, Figure 13.19;

Inputs		Outputs			
A	B	a	b	c	d
0	0	0	0	1	1
0	1	0	1	1	0
1	0	1	1	0	0
1	1	1	0	0	1

Figure 13.15

Inputs		Outputs			
A	B	a	b	c	d
0	0	0	0	1	1
0	1	0	1	1	0
1	1	1	1	0	0
1	0	1	0	0	1

Figure 13.16

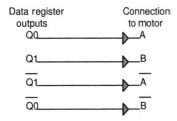

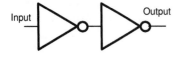

Figure 13.17 Data converter connections

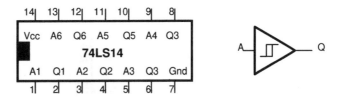

Figure 13.19 Schmitt trigger pin assignment

three of the other gates may be used as input buffers to the interface circuit if it is required to operate some distance from the computer.

Shift registers A shift register is a number of cascade connected, single-bit storage elements. Many types of bistable circuits may be used in shift registers, so long as they are connected in such a way that data only moves one element at a time, when a clock pulse is applied. Four D-type bistables, as described in Chapter 2, are shown in Figure 13.20, connected as a serial-in, parallel-out shift register.

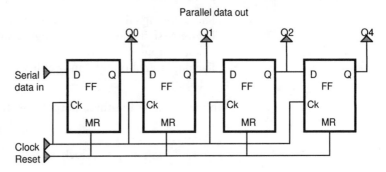

Figure 13.20 Logic circuit of a 4-bit shift register

Shift registers may either be a shift data right, a shift data left, or be reversible. Other typical applications of shift registers are:

(i) Parallel-to-serial conversion.
(ii) Multiplication and division of binary numbers by powers of 2.
(iii) Rotation of binary words (typically for stepper motor control).

The 74LS164 is an 8-bit shift register which clocks data to the right with each clock pulse; the pin assignment of this IC is shown in Figure 13.21.

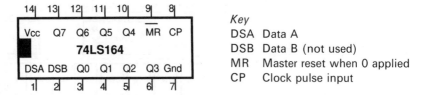

Key
DSA Data A
DSB Data B (not used)
MR Master reset when 0 applied
CP Clock pulse input

Figure 13.21 Shift register pin assignment

Figure 13.18 Delay circuit

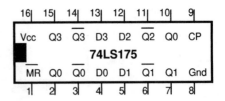

Figure 13.22   Data register pin assignment

The data register   The data register may be either 4 (Quad) or 8 (Octal) D-type bistables in one IC.

The type used in this exercise has 4 bistables with both true (Q) and complement($\overline{Q}$) outputs. The data register, Figure 13.22, is a 74LS175, which stores the data until the next data word arrives from the shift register.

Software
Develop the code which will send the three signals illustrated in Figure 13.14. Write down a 2-bit code to represent each bit to be output.

The clock signal on bit 0 is a logic 1 pulse, output   01
The reset signal on bit 1 is at logic 1 during data transmis-
    sion output   22
The data signal on bit 2 may either be at logic 0 or at logic
    1 output   00 or 44

Now combine the three outputs for transmission.

$$\text{clock} + \text{reset} + \text{data } 0 = 23$$

$$\text{clock} + \text{reset} + \text{data } 1 = 67$$

The bit-pair (ab) sequence required for clockwise rotation from Figure 13.16 is 00, 01, 11, 10. The number file required to send any bit pair is shown in Figure 13.23.

For anticlockwise rotation the bit-pair sequence is reversed. Figure 13.24 is a structure chart for this exercise, and the program is given in Listing 13.4.1.

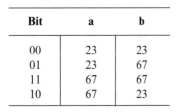

Bit	a	b
00	23	23
01	23	67
11	67	67
10	67	23

Figure 13.23   Table of numbers for bit transmission

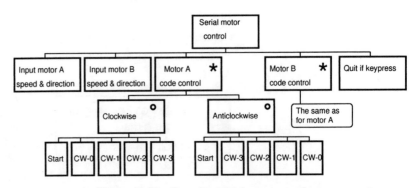

Figure 13.24   Exercise 13.4.1 structure chart

Testing the system

The hardware may be tested by connecting logic switches to act as the clock, reset and data signals. If the correct signals are input, their progress through the shift register may be monitored with a logic probe. A loop test of the complete system may be performed by connecting the outputs of the data register to the computer PPI port A. The output of the data register is then read after each code sequence has been sent.

13.4.2   Exercise – use two-conductors plus ground to control two stepper motors

This modification of the previous exercise removes the clock line from the system. It is therefore necessary to generate clock signals at the interface. A possible circuit is shown in Figure 13.25. It will be necessary to adjust the frequency of this oscillator so that it synchronises to the code for five clock pulses during code transmission. In order to maintain synchronisation it is necessary to restart the clock with each code word, this can be done by connecting the clock enable to the reset line. As it is no longer necessary to send the clock pulse, the CW file in the software should be modified.

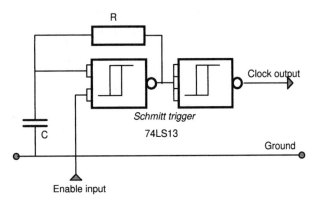

Notes
R may have a range of 1 kΩ to 4 kΩ
C should be greater than 100 nF

Figure 13.25   Clock generator circuit

13.4.3   Exercise – serial control of three stepper motors

This exercise involves adding an additional motor (C) to the hardware (no other additions are required). Another software sequence for motor C will need to be added. The code word transmitted will now be 7 bits long. The count must have time to ripple through the counter.

```
/*serialmt.c   Program for serial control of two stepper motor */
#include <stdio.h>
#include <string.h>
#include <dos.h>
void Start();
int Rotate(int);
int Control = 0x303;          /*Address of control register*/
int Out_Address = 0x301;      /*Base + 1 address*/
int Config = 0x98;            /*99 Hex configures the port as follows
                                      Port A to input
                                      Port B to output
                                      Port CL to output
                                      Port CH to input */
int hold = 1;                 /*This number controls the speed of data output*/
void main()
{
   int motorA,motorB;
   int sequenceA = 0,counterA = 0;
   int sequenceB = 0,counterB = 0;
   char Adir = 'F';
   char Bdir = 'F';
   outp(Control,Config);
   printf("\033[2JThe speed of the motors is determined by a number. The\n ");
   printf("higher the number, the slower the motor. Positive numbers\n");
   printf("cause clockwise rotation and negative numbers anticlockwise.\n\n");
   printf("Press any key to Quit when motor is running.\n");
   printf("\nInput number for Motor A ");
   scanf("%i",&motorA);
   if (motorA < 0)
   {
       motorA = motorA *-1;
       Adir = 'R';
   }
   printf("\nInput number for Motor B ");
   scanf("%i",&motorB);
   if (motorB < 0)
   {
       motorB = motorB *-1;
       Bdir = 'R';
   }
   do
   {
       Start();                      /*Reset and Start bit*/
       if (counterA == 0)            /*Motor A control*/
       {
           sequenceA++;
           counterA = motorA;
       }
```

```c
        if (sequenceA > 3 )
            sequenceA = 0;
        counterA--;
        if (Adir =='F')                /*Send Motor A bit-pair*/
            Rotate(sequenceA);
        else
            Rotate(3 - sequenceA);
        if (counterB == 0)             /*Motor B control*/
        {
            sequenceB++;
            counterB = motorB;
        }
        if (sequenceB > 3 )
            sequenceB = 0;
        counterB--;
        if (Bdir =='F')                /*Send Motor B bit-pair*/
            Rotate(sequenceB);
        else
            Rotate(3-sequenceB);
        }while(!kbhit());
    exit(1);
}
void Start()
{
    static int start[3] = {0,6,7};
    int i;
    for (i = 0; i < 3; i++)
    {
        delay(hold);
        outp(Out_Address,start[i]);
    }
}
int Rotate(int sequence)
{
    static int CW[4][4] = {2,3,2,3,      /* 0 0 */
                           3,2,6,7,      /* 0 1 */
                           6,7,6,7,      /* 1 1 */
                           6,7,2,3};     /* 1 0 */
    int i;
    for (i = 0; i < 4; i++)
    {
        delay(hold);
        outp(Out_Address,CW[sequence][i]);
    }
    return;
}
```

Listing 13.4.1   serialmt.c

14 Equipment and testing

14.1 Test equipment

14.2 Hardware problems

14.3 Testing the PPI ports

14.4 Testing the parallel printer port

14.5 Construction of LED and switch boxes

14.6 Stepper motor driver

14.7 Software problems

This chapter contains a description of the test equipment required to carry out the experiments. I have also included some testing techniques, a selection of faults and their solutions, and the construction details of the LED and switch boxes used for various experiments.

Stepper motors sold for educational purposes normally come mounted on a base with a driver IC included. However, for completeness, in Section 14.6, I have included a commercial stepper motor connected to a driver IC.

14.1 Test equipment

Power supply   Although it is possible to obtain all the voltages necessary from the computer, this can be a false economy, as short circuits can easily occur which may cause damage to the computer. A power supply with ±5 volt and ±12 volt outputs should be used to power the experimental circuits. It is well worth obtaining power supplies with output indicators, and short circuit protection. A variable 0-to-10 volt supply will also be useful.

Logic probe   An inexpensive and useful piece of equipment for quickly checking logic states. However, a voltmeter may be used if a logic probe is not available.

Multimeter   An essential instrument for fault finding. It is not necessary to have anything too elaborate, as the meter is only required for reading DC voltage up to 12 volts, and for carrying out continuity tests. Some people find an analogue meter more convenient than a digital one.

Oscilloscope (CRO)   This instrument is mainly required for checking the comparatively low frequency waveforms from the DAC exercises, so again nothing too elaborate is required.

Signal generator Only a modest signal generator is needed for the counter experiment.

Storage oscilloscope This expensive item is required for the serial port exercise in Chapter 8. As only comparatively low frequencies are to be measured, the cheapest one, consistent with any other requirements, should be selected.

14.2 Hardware problems

This section describes some typical problems and solutions.

(i) Before switching power onto a circuit always double check all connections. If possible get someone else to check.

(ii) Take care when plugging multi-pinned plugs and sockets into the computer. Always look to see that they are going in straight. It is quite easy to bend over pins and cause short circuits.

(iii) Make sure all ground connections are made good. The ground of the power supply must be connected to the ground of the computer, similarly ground terminals on switch boxes, LED boxes and instruments must all be connected to a common ground with the power supply.

(iv) When switching on a circuit for the first time, check that ICs are not getting too hot. If anything starts to smoke, switch it off immediately.

(v) Use the voltmeter to check that the DC supply is connected everywhere it should be.

(vi) Whenever possible check the hardware is working before connecting it to the computer.

(vii) Connect switch boxes to LED boxes and make sure all the switches and LEDs are working.

(viii) If the supply has an output current limiter, make sure that it is set correctly. It should act as an effective limiter, but must not cause the output voltage to fall.

(ix) Take care when removing ICs from boards or holders. I find it best to lever them out with a small screwdriver, **with the supply off**!

14.3 Testing the PPI ports

In order to test the ports for input and output it is best to use the simplest possible hardware and software. With this in mind, a number of very basic programs are provided in the following sections. The easiest way to make connections to individual pins of the ports is to use a module, similar to the one pictured in Chapter 8, available from electronics equipment suppliers.

14.3.1   Testing the PPI port for correct outputs

Figure 14.1 shows the hardware for the *output test* and Listing 14.3.1 provides for all possible conditions. Run the program three times, with the three different values for **test** as indicated in the listing.

test = 0 switches off all LEDs
test = FF switches on all LEDs
test = 55 switches on alternate LEDs.

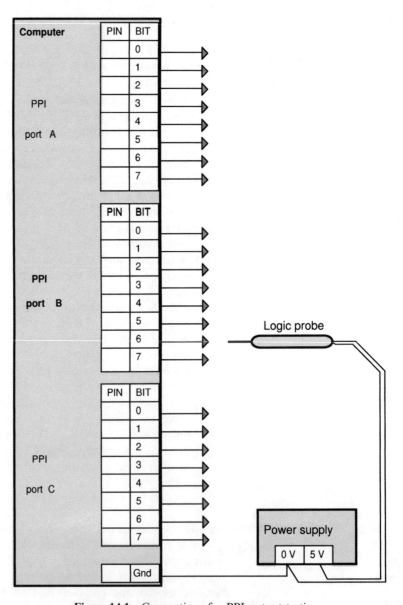

Figure 14.1   Connections for PPI output testing

```
/* ppitest1.c – all outputs to logic 0*/
#include <dos.h>              /*Required for outp() */
#include <stdio.h>            /*Required for printf()*/
int Control = 0x303;          /*Check that these addresses are correct
                                    for your machine */

int A_Address = 0x300;
int B_Address = 0x301;
int C_Address = 0x302;
int config = 0x80;            /*All ports set to output*/
int test = 0                  /* test = 0 or 0x55 or 0xFF*/
void main()
{
   outp(Control,config);
   outp(A_Address,test);
   outp(B_Address,test);
   outp(C_Address,test);
   printf("\n Outputs %0X to P P I \n",test);
}
```

Listing 14.3.1 ppitest1.c

14.3.2 Testing the PPI port for correct inputs

The hardware for this test uses a *switch box* like the one described in Section 14.5. The circuit arrangement is shown in Figure 14.2. Before commencing the test, check the switch box outputs.

Connect the switch box to each port in turn, run ppitest2.c for each port, operate each switch in turn, check that each bit can be cleared to logic 0 and set to logic 1.

```
/* ppitest2.c Input from PPI ports*/
#include <dos.h>              /*Required for outp() */
#include <stdio.h>            /*Required for printf()*/
#include <conio.h>            /*Required for gotoxy()*/
int Control = 0x303;          /*Check that these addresses are correct
                                    for your machine*/

int A_Address = 0x300;
int B_Address = 0x301;
int C_Address = 0x302;
int config = 0x9B;            /*All ports set to input*/
void main()
{
   int Y,i;
   outp(Control,config);
   printf("\n Input from PPI Ports. Press Any Key to EXIT\n");
   printf("\n  PORT A    PORT B    PORT C");
```

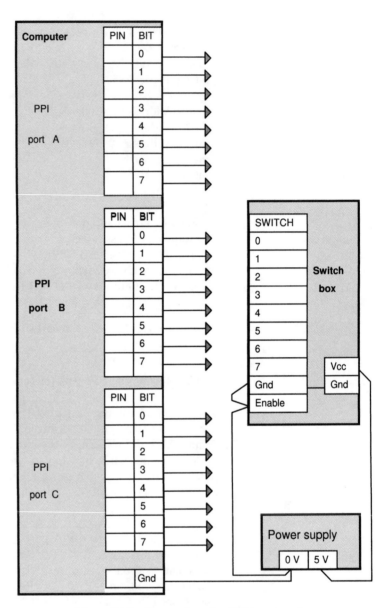

Figure 14.2   Connections for PPI input testing

```
printf("\n 7 6 5 4 3 2 1 0   7 6 5 4 3 2 1 0   7 6 5 4 3 2 1 0\n");
Y = wherey();
while(!kbhit())
{
    gotoxy(1,Y);
    for(i = 7; i > -1; i--)
        printf("%i ",((inp(A_Address) > > i)&1));
```

```
        printf(" ");
        for(i = 7; i > -1; i--)
            printf("%i ",((inp(B_Address) >> i)&1));
        printf(" ");
        for(i = 7; i > -1; i--)
            printf("%i ",((inp(C_Address) >> i)&1));
    }
}
```

Listing 14.3.2   ppitest2.c

14.4   Testing the parallel printer port

Connect the printer port as shown in Figure 14.3, run ptrtests1.c to test for correct outputs with the logic probe. Run *ptrtest1* three times with the three different values for **test** as indicated in the listing. Then run ptrtest2.c and check for correct inputs using a switch box, see Figure 14.3.

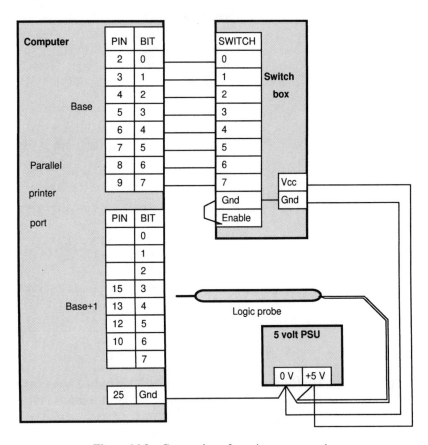

Figure 14.3   Connections for printer port testing

14.4.1   Output test software

```
/*ptrtest1.c   Output 0 to printer port*/
#include < dos.h >
#include < stdio.h >
int Out_Address = 0x3bc;     /*Insert base address of printer port*/
int test = 0;                /*test = 0, or 0X55, or 0XFF*/
void main()
{
   outp(Out_Address,test);
   printf("Output %0X to Printer Port",test);
}
```

Listing 14.4.1   ptrtest1.c

14.4.2   Input test software

```
/*ptrtest2.c   Input from Printer Port*/
#include < dos.h >
#include < stdio.h >
#include < conio.h >
int In_Address = 0x3bd;      /*Insert base address plus one*/
void main()
{
   int data,i,Y;
   printf("\n Input from Printer. Any Key to Quit");
   printf("\nThe input from pin 11 is inverted\n\n\n");
   printf("\nPins 11 10 12 13 15");
   printf("\nBits 7 6 5 4 3\n");
   Y = wherey();
   while(!kbhit())
   {
      data = inp(In_Address);
      gotoxy(9,Y);
      for(i = 7; i > 2; i--)
         printf(" %i ",(data > >i)&1);
   }
}
```

Listing 14.4.2   ptrtest2.c

14.5   Construction of LED and switch boxes

Two items which are required for many exercises are a **light emitting diode (LED)** box for use as an output indicator, and a **switch** box to supply inputs. An example of each device is provided in the following subsections. An alternative arrangement is to use a combined LED and switch box as described in Section 14.5.3.

14.5.1   The LED box

The LED box basically consists of eight terminals and eight LEDs. However, some form of buffer is required between the terminals and the LEDs so that the box does not load[1] circuits when it is connected. There are two alternative circuits. Figure 14.4 shows an LED being driven from a logic gate. Eight of these circuits are required.

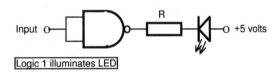

Figure 14.4   Driving an LED from a NAND gate

This is the preferred way of driving an LED from a TTL NAND gate output. The light level produced by the LED depends upon the forward current, which may be in the range 1 mA to 40 mA. An ordinary TTL device can sink[2] 16 mA in the logic 0 state. This gives a minimum value of R of 220 Ω.

Components required for LEDs driven by NAND gates:

Quantity	Item
2	7400, Quad, 2 input NAND gates
8	220 Ω resistors
8	LEDs
10	Terminals
	Strip-board or proto-board

Figure 14.5 shows the eight LEDs connected to an Octal common emitter Darlington driver (ULN2803A).

Components required for Darlington driver, Figure 14.5:

Quantity	Item
1	2803A Darlington driver
8	220 Ω resistors
8	LEDs
10	Terminals
	Strip-board or proto-board

---

[1] Loading in this sense causes additional current to be taken from the circuit output which could cause false operation.

[2] Sink used in this way means 'pass' or 'conduct' safely.

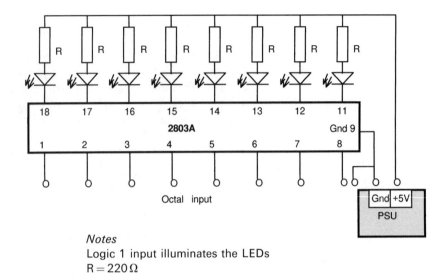

Notes
Logic 1 input illuminates the LEDs
R = 220 Ω

Figure 14.5   Octal driver LED box circuit

14.5.2   The switch box

A suitable circuit of a switch box is shown in Figure 14.6. This uses a 74LS245, see Chapter 2 for pin assignment. To increase the usefulness of the switch box an enable terminal is incorporated. The enable terminal should be connected to ground when not required.

Components required for switch box, Figure 14.6:

Quantity	Item
1	74LS245
8	1 kΩ resistors
8	SPST switches
12	Terminals
	Strip-board or proto-board

14.5.3   Economy LED/switch box

Figure 14.8 is a circuit of an economy version of the switch box, using an 8-bit DIL switch. LEDs have been incorporated to provide both input and output indication. In the circuit LED A is illuminated when the switches are disabled. A picture of the constructed circuit is illustrated in Figure 14.7.

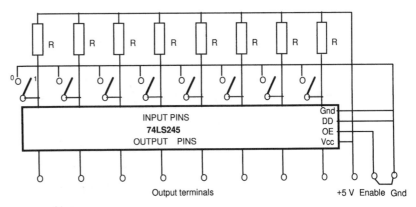

Notes

R = 1 kΩ

Logic 0 on Output when a switch is closed

Figure 14.6 Switch Box Circuit

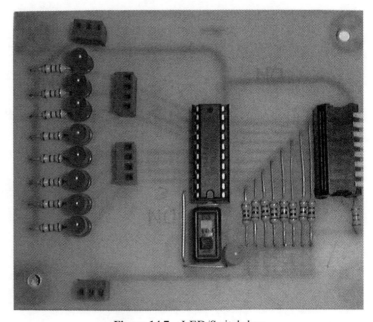

Figure 14.7 LED/Switch box

14.6 Stepper motor driver

Motors sold for educational purposes usually come mounted with a driver IC. If a commercial motor is used, Figure 14.10 shows how it may be connected to an L283E stepper motor driver IC. Details of the motor connections should be supplied with the motor.

14.7 Software problems

This final section deals with software run time problems. Clearly the software must compile satisfactorily in order to produce an executable file (name.EXE).

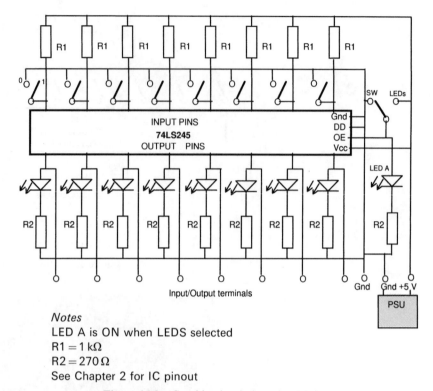

Notes
LED A is ON when LEDS selected
R1 = 1 kΩ
R2 = 270 Ω
See Chapter 2 for IC pinout

Figure 14.8   Combined switch and LED box

Figure 14.9   Commercial stepper motor

It is important to take care of your programs. Use at least two discs, one for program development and the other as a back-up which contains completed work. It can be heart-breaking to have all your programs on one disc which has become faulty and cannot be read. Remember discs are very delicate and should always be transported in boxes.

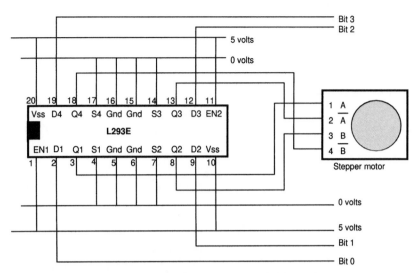

Figure 14.10 Stepper motor and driver IC

The following is a list of points which should be considered when things go wrong:

(i) When there is no output from an interface a quick solution is often to try the interface on another machine. **BEWARE OF THIS PRACTICE!** A faulty interface can damage all the available machines. However, it is a good idea to check and exchange connecting cables.

(ii) If the output from a port is not as expected, substitute printf() statements for outp() and see what is sent to the screen.

(iii) If the input from a port is not as expected, substitute getch() statements for inp() to see if the program is inputting as expected.

(iv) Most compilers allow the program to be stepped through, executing one instruction at a time. This is useful for finding out where a program is 'hung up'. Variables may also be inspected during this process.

(v) Again it should be emphasised that a missing ground will produce odd results. Sometimes only a few conditions will appear peculiar, such as when the input is 0s or all 1s.

Bibliography

Black, Ulysses D. (1989) *Data Networks*. Prentice Hall

Coleman, Derek (1994) *Object-oriented Development*. Prentice Hall

Dewar, R. B. K. and Smosna, M. (1990) *Microprocessors: A Programmer's View*. McGraw-Hill

Mano, M. M. (1993) *Computer Systems Architecture*. Prentice Hall

Mitchell (1986) *32-bit Microprocessors*. Collins

Waite, Mitchell and Prata, Stephen (1990) *New C Primer Plus*. Howard W. Sams & Co.

Waites, Nick and Knot, Geoffrey (1990) *A Level, BTEC and First Degree Computing*. Business Education Publisher Ltd

Whitworth, Ian R. (1984) *16-bit Microprocessors*. Collins

Wilkinson (1987) *Digital Design Systems*. Prentice Hall

Zaks, Rodnay (1982) *Programming the Z80*. Sybex

Manufacturers' literature

(1993) 80C51-Based 8-Bit Microcontrollers. North American Philips Corporation

(1998) TMS329 DSP Product Overview. Texas Instruments

(1995) Z80 Microprocessor Family. Zilog

(1987) Microsoft MS-DOS User's Guide and User's Reference. Microsoft Corporation.

Index